Creationism Versus Evolution

Other books in the At Issue series:

At ✳ Issue

Creationism Versus Evolution

Eric Braun, *Book Editor*

Bruce Glassman, *Vice President*
Bonnie Szumski, *Publisher*
Helen Cothran, *Managing Editor*

GREENHAVEN PRESS
An imprint of Thomson Gale, a part of The Thomson Corporation

THOMSON
━━━━✳━━━━™
GALE

Detroit • New York • San Francisco • San Diego • New Haven, Conn.
Waterville, Maine • London • Munich

For more information, contact
Greenhaven Press
27500 Drake Rd.
Farmington Hills, MI 48331-3535
Or you can visit our Internet site at http://www.gale.com

LIBRARY OF CONGRESS CATALOGING-IN-PUBLICATION DATA

Creationism versus evolution / Eric Braun, book editor.
 p. cm. — (At issue)
Includes bibliographical references and index.
ISBN 0-7377-2703-9 (lib. : alk. paper) — ISBN 0-7377-2704-7 (pbk. : alk. paper)
 1. Creationism. 2. Evolution—Religious aspects. 3. Intelligent design
(Teleology) I. Title: Creationism versus evolution. II. Braun, Eric, 1971– . III. At
issue (San Diego, Calif.)
BS652.C74 2005
231.7'652—dc22   2004060631

Printed in the United States of America

Contents

Introduction

In 1859 Charles Darwin published his classic work *On the Origin of Species*, in which he introduced his theory of natural selection, the process by which living organisms evolve (commonly known as evolution, although Darwin avoided this term for most of his life). The work revolutionized the biological sciences and ignited a storm of controversy that continues to the present day, pitting modern scientific inquiry against traditional religious belief.

According to Darwin, living organisms pass on innumerable traits to their offspring, with random, minute variations. The offspring that live long enough to reproduce tend to be the ones that have inherited variations that make them better suited to their specific environment and better able to compete for limited resources; that is, the fittest organisms survive. Different random variations make new generations of offspring adapt, or fail to adapt, to different environments and changing conditions. Thus, species naturally change and diverge, evolve into new species, and die out, a process Darwin suggested took eons, based on geological evidence and the fossil record.

From the start, Darwin's most vocal opponents believed evolution directly threatened the authority of the Christian religion, based on biblical revelations about the creation of the world and humans' place in the hierarchy of God's creatures. The book of Genesis relates that God created Earth and all its life forms, complete according to God's design, in six days. Many Christians of Darwin's day interpreted this account literally and adhered to the time line created in the 1650s by Irish archbishop James Ussher, who calculated the age of Earth based on the life spans of biblical figures, beginning with the first humans, Adam and Eve. By this calculation, Earth was only about six thousand years old.

Many devout Christians also believed modern species existed as God created them, each fitting a particular purpose in a divine scheme that ordained humankind as the most noble of God's creations. The concept that humans evolved from other, lower life forms, or that a species changed because it was somehow not suited to its environment, offended Christians who perceived in Darwin's theory a blasphemous implication that God's plan was somehow not perfect.

By the end of the nineteenth century, however, the weight of scientific evidence that Earth was 4.5 to 5 billion years old had persuaded most Christians that evolution was not incompatible with their Christian beliefs. They simply regarded the creation story in the Bible as symbolic, rather than literal, and accepted scientific evidence that the first life on Earth appeared about 2.5 billion years ago, and that living organisms evolved from primordial, single-cell life forms.

A significant fundamendalist faction continued to deny evidence supporting evolution, such as the discovery of skeletal remains of extinct, intermediate species linking known species. Their argument was simple: If you believed in the Bible then you could not believe in evolution. There was no philosophical common ground. The primary battlefield became the curricula of public schools. Fundamentalists opposed teaching children subject matter that seemed to directly contradict the Bible. Instead, they advocated teaching creationism, the theory that God created the world and all life within it, and insisted creationism was no less valid a theory than evolution. Several states, especially in the Bible Belt of the South, forbade the teaching of evolution.

The Twentieth-Century Dominance of Evolution in the Curricula

The face of the creationism-evolution argument would change soon after World War II (1939–1945), when the United States became involved in the Cold War with its rival, the Soviet Union. Both superpowers competed for military and technological superiority, which led President Dwight D. Eisenhower to declare a new American focus on scientific research. He channeled significant federal funding to American schools specifically for science education, including the teaching of evolution, which by then was viewed by scientists as the very backbone of biology. In 1968, the U.S. Supreme Court declared unconstitutional any state law that forbade the teaching of evolution.

Now that creationists could not prevent students from learning about evolution, they changed their approach in the battle for school curricula. They proposed laws in many states that creationism and evolution should both be taught as competing theories. Court challenges limited that tactic, however, because creationism was faith based and the constitutional separation of church and state effectively kept religious teaching out of public schools.

However, by the 1960s a new creationist movement was gaining popularity: creation science. Creation scientists submit that the creation story of the Bible can be supported with scientific evidence. The movement was spearheaded by a 1961 book, *The Genesis Flood,* by professor of religion John C. Whitcomb Jr. and hydraulic engineer Henry M. Morris. *The Genesis Flood* sought to prove scientifically that Noah's flood, described in Genesis, was an actual historical catastrophic event. The authors believed that evidence of the flood's scientific validity would open the door to scientific acceptance of other biblical accounts, including the origins of life described in Genesis.

Others had made this argument before—most notably a Seventh-day Adventist named George McCready Price. Whitcomb's and Morris's academic credentials—both held doctoral degrees—far outshone Price's, and they gained much more serious attention. *The Genesis Flood* created a sensation among conservative Christians.

The battle went back to the classrooms again—now creationists argued they had a scientific claim to a place in science class curricula. Their argument was that evolution was "just a theory," and that as a competing scientific theory, creation science should be taught along with it. They also maintained that evolution should be considered a religion because it was a theory on the origin of life. Therefore, teaching evolution and not creationism violated the Establishment Clause of the Constitution, which prohibited governments from favoring one religion over another.

Arkansas and Louisiana passed laws in 1981 that would have required the teaching of creationism in public schools. But courts declared the laws unconstitutional, stating that the theory of evolution was scientific, not religious. The courts also said that creationism was a religious explanation of life and that the Arkansas and Louisiana laws were therefore unconstitutional because they favored one religion over another.

The Intelligent Design Movement

Creation scientists shifted their focus in the 1990s to local school boards, where they have presented purportedly scientific results of studies into creationism and urged curriculum committees to "teach the controversy" between the competing theories of origins. The most significant development in the debate, however, is the rise of the so-called intelligent design (ID) movement in the 1990s. ID theorists, like creation scientists, argue from a scientific standpoint, though their argument is much more sophisticated. ID theorists such as Michael Behe and William Dembski use principles of molecular biology and mathematical probability, respectively, to make the case that life is too complex to have evolved. Behe's theory of irreducible complexity is an elaborate argument that certain biological systems, such as the bacterial flagellum, could not have evolved from simpler forms through numerous, successive, slight modifications (requirements of Darwinism) because if any one part is changed or taken away, the whole system fails. Each part of the system is required to make it work, so the system had to appear as a whole system.

Behe argues that these systems were necessarily created, intact, by an intelligent designer. Most ID theorists avoid naming the designer as God, and they reject the label of creationist. Also, most ID theorists allow that Earth is old and that a great deal of evolution does occur, particularly microevolution—minor change within a species or small group of organisms. They deny macroevolution, large changes over a long period of time that can produce entirely new species.

The shift in creationists' attack from philosophical to scientific has raised the stakes over the future of science and science education in the United States. A great flurry of new debate has erupted in recent years, as evolutionists have felt compelled to defend evolution more fervently than ever before. They continue to argue that creationism, including ID, is not science and permitting it in science curricula undermines the science education that students need.

Whichever side one comes down on in this debate, one positive outcome is evident. All sides have been forced to look harder at their beliefs, how they came to them, and to confront whether their beliefs affect their findings or their findings affect their beliefs. *At Issue: Creationism Versus Evolution* provides a snapshot of those beliefs and the arguments being made to defend them.

1

Evolution Alone Explains Life on Earth

Massimo Pigliucci

Massimo Pigliucci is associate professor of ecology and evolution at the University of Tennessee, Knoxville. He holds a master's degree in biological sciences and doctorates in genetics and botany. Pigliucci was the recipient of the 1997 Dobzhansky Award from the Society for the Study of Evolution.

Any credible theory of life on Earth must withstand scientific scrutiny based on asking a specific question, answering it with a hypothesis based on observation and experimentation, and then testing that hypothesis to try to disprove it. There is only one theory of evolution, answering the question "How do species originate and change?" The theory has survived more than one hundred years of such scrutiny. In contrast, although creationists try to present a unified front, there is a wide range of creationist positions—from flat-earth literalists to more liberal creationist positions that graft evolution onto theistic origins, or try to equate biblical "days" and geological ages and then claim their theory is scientific. No creationist theory holds up to the scientific method, but creationists are interested in winning an ideological war, not in scientific evidence. Creationists start with a preferred conclusion (God created life) and then make observations about the natural world that fit that theory, ignoring or discounting contradictory evidence. Human progress depends on a scientific, not theological, understanding of life on Earth, and only evolution provides that.

There is one theory of evolution, just as there is one theory of general relativity in physics. True, there are different schools of evolutionary thought that emphasize distinct mechanisms to explain organic evolution, and creationists have tried to capitalize on these differences to show that the whole field is in disarray. Yet differences among scientists are the bread and butter of scientific progress. It is through the empirically driven resolution of theoretical disagreements [the resolution of disagreements through testing and observation] that science at its best progresses and yields a better understanding of the natural world. . . . But the realities of scientific practice and discourse are far from what creationist propaganda claims. Furthermore, the idea of a monolithic and unchangeable science is a dangerous myth—one that scientists and science educators should work toward eradicating.

> *The realities of scientific practice and discourse are far from what creationist propaganda claims.*

On the other hand, even a superficial look at creationism itself clearly shows that creationists have gone to a great deal of trouble to construct what looks deceptively like a unified front to naïve outsiders. As we shall see, the difference between proponents of intelligent design theory such as [American mathematician] William Dembski and young-Earth creationists like [American biochemist] Duane Gish spans a theological and scientific abyss. One of the few things that these people have in common is their hatred for what they perceive as a materialistic, scientific worldview that leaves no space for God and spirituality. Intelligent design defender Phillip Johnson has proposed the idea that creationists can win by driving a wedge into what he thinks is a small but crucial crack in the edifice of science. . . . I would like to suggest to scientists and educators that the crack in the *creationist* camp is much wider and easier to exploit, if only we stop being on the defensive and initiate a counterattack. . . . I will first briefly discuss the astounding variety of creationist positions, focusing in particular on the two most popular ones as embodied by the Institute for Creation Research and by the Discovery Institute and its Center for the

Renewal of Science and Culture. As a counterpoint, I will then explain what evolutionary theory is really about. . . .

The Many Forms of Creationism

Perhaps the best classification of positions on the question of *origins,* as the broader conception of evolution is often referred to, has been proposed by [American biologist] Eugenie Scott of the National Center for Science Education and is summarized in the figure below. As Scott points out, there [are many] ideas to choose from, and they differ in degree as to what they accept from science on the one hand and from the Bible on the other.

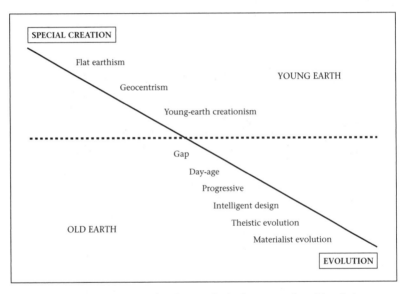

At one extreme we find people believing that Earth is actually flat. While these are certainly a minority even among creationists, their thoroughly literalist position is arguably the most biblical of them all: In addition to rejecting evolution, they believe not only that Earth is 6,000 years old, but that it is flat and is the center of the universe, precisely as the Bible says.

A slightly different position is the geocentric one, which accepts the idea of a spherical Earth but squarely rejects astronomy after Copernicus and Galilei. This is also a minority view, but it is instructive—together with the flat-Earth position—because it is indicative of an interesting aspect of mainstream creationist thinking. On many occasions I have had conversations or have exchanged letters with young-Earth creationists (the next group in Scott's classification) who vehemently deny being gullible, antiscience individuals. They claim that the *scientific* evidence is definitely against evolution and in favor of a young Earth. I usually politely point out that the only reason they think so is that they believe . . . the Bible [to be error free] in scientific as well as spiritual matters. I then occasionally ask why they don't believe that Earth stands still while the sun moves around it and that our planet is flat, since both notions are also present in the Bible. In fact, one could argue that these two positions are much more clearly defined in the Christian scriptures than the age of Earth, which has to be calculated on the basis of assumptions concerning the life span of the lines of descent mentioned in the book. The astonishing creationist response is to deny that the Bible makes claims either about a flat Earth or in defense of geocentrism. But this goes clearly against not only the existence of creationists who see and defend both claims, but also against the historical evidence: For most of Western history, Christians have espoused both views precisely on biblical grounds! It is not for nothing that both Copernicus and Galilei got into trouble with the Church of Rome.

> *At one extreme we find people believing that Earth is actually flat.*

Young-Earth creationists, however, seem to be able to live with this internal contradiction; they actually represent the majority of creationists in the United States (according to a 1999 Gallup poll, 45 percent of Americans believe that God created human beings "pretty much in (their) present form at one time or another within the last 10,000 years"). For them the story in Genesis is to be taken literally: The world was created 6,000 years ago, and most humans and animals died in a worldwide flood that occurred about 4,000 years ago. . . . Several interesting fallacies underlie this position, and young-Earth creationists are the epitome of what happens when science education fails completely. It simply makes no sense—given the evidence that we have today from a variety of fields, such as geology, paleontology, ecology, physics, and astronomy—to deny that Earth is billions of years old and that while mass extinctions certainly occurred, they were not due to floods and no such event happened on a worldwide basis so recently in Earth's history.

Old-Earth Creationism

The next category in Scott's classification of theories of origins marks a fundamental theological, if not yet scientific, divide from the positions discussed so far: We are now entering the realm of *old-Earth creationism*, which therefore at least acknowledges modern geology. . . . It is also in agreement with the scientific research in this field conducted throughout the twentieth century. Within old-Earth creationism, the idea often referred to as *gap theory* is by far the most peculiar. Supporters maintain that there is a large temporal [time] gap between the first and second chapters of Genesis in the Hebrew Bible, suggesting the existence of a pre-Adamic Earth that was destroyed and replaced by a second creation, when God started over and (re?)made Adam and Eve. This interpretation obviously solves the well-known problem posed by the discrepancy between the two accounts of creation in Genesis, but literalists are clearly less than happy with such a solution because it is obtained at the theologically costly price of introducing a scenario (two successive creations) of which there is no hint in the Bible itself. This is the much-dreaded "slippery slope" of interpretation of the sacred Scripture that, even though it is adopted in one fashion or another by most practicing Christians, is seen as very dangerous by fundamentalists, who believe that the word of God should be a clear and universal message, not subject to the whims and fashions of human explanations.

> **//** *Young-Earth creationists are the epitome of what happens when science education fails completely.* **//**

An even more liberal interpretation of the Bible is adopted by people espousing the next category of old-Earth creationism in Scott's taxonomy: the day-age system. According to this idea, each "day" referred to in the traditional six-day account of creation is comparable to a geological age, so it literally took tens of millions of years to create stars, planets, and life on Earth—

in convenient agreement with the evidence from astronomy and geology. This solution still suffers some obvious shortcomings from a scientific standpoint, most egregiously the incompatibility between the chronology of events in Genesis (e.g., whales before land animals) and the data from the fossil record. But it also makes religious fundamentalists very unhappy because it proceeds further down the slippery slope of arbitrary interpretation of the Bible: What is there to stop the believer from even accepting a substantial amount of evolution?

> // Old-Earth creationism . . . *at least acknowledges modern geology.* //

Not much, as is clear from a cursory examination of the next position: so-called progressive creationism. A typical proponent of this version of old-Earthism is Hugh Ross of Reasons To Believe ministries, which, as the name implies is based on the idea that someone can accept Christianity on the basis of *reason* not just on faith. Progressive creationism is a peculiar and idiosyncratic blend of creationism and science that accepts, for example, the Big Bang and many other scientific conclusions, even within the biological sciences, but limits the power of evolution. For example, evolution is said to occur, but only within the basic "kinds" of organisms originally created by God. Although many young-Earth creationists, such as Duane Gish, also allow what they refer to as *microevolution* within kinds, progressive creationists—because they accept long spans of geological time—at least don't find themselves in the awkward position of having to concede more evolution than even the most ardent evolutionist would feel comfortable with (the number of "kinds" was limited by the size of Noah's Ark for a young-Earth creationist, so tens of millions of species had to evolve from a few thousand in as little as 4,000 years: an *astronomic* evolutionary rate by any standard!).

Working our way through Scott's useful classification, we finally arrive at intelligent design (ID) theory. . . . This is the idea—originally formulated in some detail by the ancient Greeks—that the universe is the result of some kind of supernatural plan evidently constrained by forces that even the gods cannot entirely control. Plato, in the *Timaeus*, presents us with the idea of a god (later called the *demiurge*, literally "the craftsman") which makes the universe "as best as it can be" made within the constraints imposed by contingency. . . .

> **"** *The chronology of events in Genesis (e.g., whales before land animals) and the data from the fossil record [are incompatible].* **"**

The last step in this long series of creationist positions is usually referred to as *theistic evolution.* This is the position more or less implicitly accepted by the majority of Christians, especially in western European countries: Simply put, God works through the natural laws and processes that He created, and there is no reason to think that natural selection is an exception. This is also essentially the official position of the Catholic Church after two writings of Pope John Paul II. Previous popes, such as Pius XII had taken a stern position against evolutionary theory: "Some imprudently and indiscreetly hold that evolution . . . explains the origin of all things. . . . Communists gladly subscribe to this opinion so that when the souls of man have been deprived of every idea of a personal God, they may the more efficaciously defend and propagate their dialectical materialism." John Paul II (the pope who, without being a paragon of liberalism, still managed to pardon Galilei, albeit after a few centuries of delay), on the contrary, wrote a much more sober letter in 1997 to the Pontifical Academy of Sciences stating that "new knowledge has led to the recognition of the theory of evolution as more than a hypothesis.". . .

Materialistic Evolution

The last entry in Scott's classification is the only one that does not involve any creationist component at all, even of the mild type accepted by the Catholic Church and most mainstream Protestant denominations: the much-dreaded (by all creationists) materialistic evolution. This is a *philosophical* (as opposed to scientific) position maintaining that there is no reason whatsoever to invoke supramaterial causes for any natural law or process, including evolution. Not even the most ardent Christian would submit that God works directly through the law of gravity by supervising the motion of every single object; analogously, biologists tend to think that natural selection is just that—a *natural* process with no need of supervision.

Two things are important to realize in connection with materialistic evolution. First, and perhaps most importantly for our discussion and for the creation-evolution controversy, even materialistic evolution does not automatically imply atheism. There are several more possibilities that permit acceptance of both materialistic evolution and belief in a god. This is true both in theory and in practice. In theory, for example, one can be a deist—that is, somebody who believes that God created the universe and its laws but then refrained from any further direct intervention in His creation. In practice, Theodosius Dobzhansky, the evolutionist responsible for one of the sentences most hated by creationists ("nothing in biology makes sense if not in the light of evolution") was himself a devout Christian. Second, it has always been commonly accepted that most scientists are materialists and do not believe in a personal god. This turns out to be quantitatively accurate. . . . Surveys show that such is the belief (or more properly lack thereof) of a majority of "average" scientists and of almost every "top" scientist (as measured by their membership in the National Academy of Sciences). . . .

> **// Biologists tend to think that natural selection is just that—a natural *process with no need of* supervision. //**

Given the [huge variety] of opinion regarding important conceptual issues within the creationist camp, . . . it is amazing that creationists can present such a unified front. . . . Or is this unified front just a matter of appearances, thinly disguising the vat of trouble that is brewing among creationists? . . .

An Ideological War

Scientists and educators are involved in this debate because they care about science education, not about winning an ideological war. In this, I can safely say, they are different from creationists. Even though most creationists are sincerely convinced of their positions, they are interested only in winning the ideological war. If evolutionary theory had no theological implications (say, like atomic theory), there would be no debate. This point is strangely missed by scientists, who continue to behave as if creationists were either lunatics (which by and large they are not) or as if they needed to be rebutted on solid scientific grounds, after which they would go away.

> *If evolutionary theory had no theological implications (say, like atomic theory), there would be no debate.*

The reason it is important to explain science to the general public is that it is important for our society that people have a scientific understanding of the world. Without it, as a recent report of the National Science Foundation remarked, people are likely to make bad decisions in the voting booth, as members of a jury, or in their private lives when considering an insurance policy or a moneymaking scheme. But to refuse to accept that this particular debate is about ideology rather than science is foolish and largely accounts for the lack of progress we have made since the Scopes trial.[1] It is therefore urgent that scientists and educators be in a position to counterattack and to point out the internal inconsistencies in the creationist camp. As uncomfortable as this may be, this is bound to make much more of an immediate impact than any esoteric explanation of the second principle of thermodynamics. . . .

What Evolution Really Is

Having attempted to explain the basic tenets of the major forms of creationism, it is only fair—and most urgent, judging from my experiences at debates against creationists—to briefly explain what evolutionary theory really is, and even a few things that it is thought to be but isn't. . . . The evolution-creation debate is marred by many misunderstandings and a lot of ideological posturing, often on both sides. One major thing that creationists

1. the 1925 trial of John T. Scopes, who was found guilty of violating Tennessee law that prohibited the teaching of evolution in public schools

seem reluctant to acknowledge, however, is the distinction be-tween what evolutionary theory actually is and what they think it is. And the difference is both huge and crucial. No matter what one's ideological position, it seems to me necessary to under-stand what *biologists* claim evolution to be and not to build straw men just to be able to demonize the opposition. . . .

If one asks an evolutionary biologist—by definition the only person qualified to answer the question—she will tell you that evolution is simply a change of gene frequencies over time. This may sound rather simple and philosophically unin-teresting, but it is in line with what science is all about: seeking answers to specific questions, not to questions of ultimate meaning. The theory of genetic changes in natural populations is very well understood by a branch of biology called popula-tion genetics, and modern molecular biology provides direct evidence that gene frequencies do indeed change under our very nose. Examples are abundant and are found in all classes of living organisms (humans included, of course). . . .

Yet most people think of evolution in terms of *descent with modification*, to use Darwin's term, of large organisms, and in particular animals. . . . Let's look at evolution seen at the level of macroscopic creatures and long timescales. This is the realm of comparative anatomy and paleontology, and the evidence for evolution of plants and animals comes from studies of their ge-netics, physiology, morphology, and development. Additional evidence comes from the much maligned fossil record. . . .

It is therefore urgent that scientists and educators . . . point out the internal inconsistencies in the creationist camp.

There are many great examples of morphological evolution in plants and animals, but perhaps one of the most spectacular is the evolution of modern whales, which has recently been largely elucidated by a series of paleontological findings and molecular studies. . . .

The story of whales started about 55 million years ago, al-though the exact group of ancestors is currently unknown. They were terrestrial animals belonging to the Artiodactyla (the mod-ern group that includes hippopotami, sheep, camels, and pigs).

That group was itself closely related to the now extinct Mesony-chia, which until recently were considered a better candidate for the direct ancestors of whales, but are now regarded as their cousins. The earliest animals belonging to the Cetacea (of which modern whales and dolphins are also members) were closely re-lated to *Pakicetus* and *Ambulocetus*. . . . The early relatives of these two were terrestrial artiodactyls, occupying an ecological niche similar to the one filled today by bears (i.e., they were probably scavengers and fish eaters), although whales and bears them-selves are not closely related to each other. Between 53 and 45 million years ago (MYA) a variety of intermediate forms appeared to connect the artiodactyl ancestors to modern whales. Some of these forms have been found in the fossil record, though there probably were many more that did not survive the fossilization process. Fifty MYA the already mentioned *Pakicetus* appeared, sporting a lifestyle that included both land and water hunting (judging from its skeleton and skull). A little after that, *Ambulo-cetus* showed advanced features adapted to a marine life, with a skeleton very similar to that of modern otters, sea lions, and other pinnipeds that are still today in an intermediate stage of their aquatic evolution. Between 40 and 35 MYA other forms arose, in particular *Basilosaurus*. This animal was truly almost like a whale except for the still apparent limbs, which, however, were reduced enough to make it impossible for it to walk on land.

What Evolution Is Not

So much for what evolution *is*. Now there are a couple of im-portant things that evolution is *not*, misleading claims by cre-ationists notwithstanding. For example, evolution is not a the-ory of the origin of life, for the simple reason that evolution deals with changes in living organisms induced by a combina-tion of random (mutation) and nonrandom (natural selection) forces. By definition, before life originated there were no muta-tions, and therefore there was no variation; hence, natural se-lection could not possibly have acted. This means that the ori-gin of life is a (rather tough) problem for physics and chemistry to deal with, but not a proper area of inquiry for evolutionary biology. It would be like asking a geologist to explain the origin of planets: The geologist's work starts *after* planets come into ex-istence, and it is the cosmologist who deals with the question of planetary origins. . . .

Evolution is also most definitely *not* a theory of the origin of the universe. As interesting as this question is, it is rather the realm of physics and cosmology. Mutation and natural selection, the mechanisms of evolution, do not have anything to do with stars and galaxies. It is true that some people, even astronomers, refer to the "evolution" of the universe, but this is meant in the general sense of change through time, not the technical sense of the Darwinian theory. That the universe does "evolve" in this larger sense is clear from the fact that powerful telescopes like the Hubble can actually peer into the distant past (thanks to the fact that light travels at a finite speed) and show us firsthand what primordial galaxies looked like. . . .

> *Evolution is simply a change of gene frequencies over time. . . . [This definition] is in line with what science is all about: seeking answers to specific questions, not to questions of ultimate meaning.*

Is the fact that evolutionary theory can explain neither the origin of life nor the formation of the universe a "failure" of Darwinian evolution? Of course not. To apply evolutionary biology to those problems is like mixing apples and oranges, or like trying to understand a basketball play by applying the rules of baseball. Creationists often do this, but their doing so betrays either a fundamental misunderstanding of science or a good dose of intellectual dishonesty—neither of which should be condoned.

Creationists and scientists think along vastly different lines. . . . Creationist decisions are based on beliefs and preferences, not on any attempt to objectively assess the problem. As I said earlier, creationists—contrary to all principles of sound science and critical thinking—start out with a preferred conclusion and then try to find evidence to back it up. . . . This is exactly the modus operandi of pseudoscience and what, in the words of philosopher of science Karl Popper, distinguishes it from actual science.

2

Creationism Explains Life on Earth

Benjamin D. Wiker

Benjamin D. Wiker is a senior fellow in the Center for Science and Culture at the Discovery Institute, a center for challenging Darwinism and developing Intelligent Design, located in Seattle, Washington. He is the author of Moral Darwinism: How We Became Hedonists. *He is a lecturer in theology and science at Franciscan University of Steubenville, Ohio.*

In spite of critics' claims that it is repackaged creationism—that it is religious and not scientific—the Intelligent Design (ID) movement is in fact a welcome and inevitable scientific revolution. The natural world provides abundant reasons to doubt evolutionary theory as well as abundant evidence that life on Earth was created by an intelligent designer. ID affirms microevolution (evolution that results in change in populations at the species level or smaller), which can be confirmed by science, but denies macroevolution (evolution that results in large-scale changes such as species formation), which cannot. The sudden appearance of nearly all modern living phyla during the Cambrian era (as shown in the fossil record) shows that modern life did not evolve slowly. Furthermore, the conditions necessary for the first living cells to arise would require a miracle. A designer explains these things, while evolution does not.

It may well be the most important Intellectual movement to occur in the last 200 years, if not the last half-millennium. Its roots are in the sciences, but when it reaches full flower, it may

Benjamin D. Wiker, "Does Science Point to God? The Intelligent Design Revolution," *Crisis Magazine*, April 7, 2003, pp. 1–8. Copyright © 2001 by *Crisis Magazine*, Washington, DC, USA. Reproduced by permission.

branch into nearly every discipline, from theology, philosophy, and the social sciences to history and literature, and redefine almost every aspect of culture, from morality and law to the arts.

It's the Intelligent Design (ID) movement, and it's reshaping the face of science.

> *The [Intelligent Design] movement seeks to restore sanity to science, philosophy, and hence culture.*

The revolution began in the latter half of the 20th century as a result of discoveries in the various sciences that seemed to point to an intelligent being as the cause of nature's amazing intricacies. The aim of ID is included in its origin: the ever-deeper investigation of nature to uncover every aspect of its stunningly contrived complexity. Such complexity is the sure sign of intentional design, and the discovery and contemplation of it is also the natural delight of our intellect.

The ID movement directly contradicts the modern secularist [nonreligious] intellectual trend that has so thoroughly dominated Western culture for the last two centuries (even though this trend began 500 years ago, in the early Renaissance). Although this secularization has reached nearly every aspect of our culture, its source of authority has always been in a kind of philosophic and scientific alliance.

Evidence of a Designer

In philosophy, the secularized intellect denies the existence of any truth beyond what is humanly contrived. . . . The secularization of science manifests itself in the belief that nature has no need for an intelligent designer but is self-caused and self-contained. Secularized science has as its aim the reduction of apparent design, whether cosmological or biological, to the unintelligent interplay of chance and brute necessity (either the necessity of law or of the physical constituents). Since nature itself has no intrinsic order, then (by default) the human intellect is the only source of intellectual order. Secularized science thus supports secularized philosophy, and secularized philosophy functions as the articulate mouthpiece of the alliance.

The ID movement seeks to restore sanity to science, philosophy, and hence culture by investigating the possibility that nature, rather than being the result of unintelligent, purposeless forces, can only be understood as the effect of an Intelligent Designer. But again, to say that the ID revolution contradicts the claims of secularized science does not mean that the contradiction arises from some contrariety or conspiracy on the part of ID proponents. It arises from the evidence of nature itself, and the ID movement is merely pointing to the evidence nature has provided (even while, as an active mode of scientific inquiry, it seeks to uncover more). In science, it points to the growing evidence of intelligent fine tuning, both cosmological and biological, and to the various failures of secularized science to make good its claims that the order of nature can be completely reduced to unintelligent causes. As more and more evidence is gathered, secularized philosophy will be forced to confront the scientific evidence that truth is not, after all, a mere human artifact, because a designing intellect has provided the amazingly intricate beings and laws to which the scientific intellect must conform if it is truly to have scientia—a knowledge of nature. Soon enough, secularized culture will be compelled to realign.

Criticism of ID

That is not, however, the story you will hear from the critics of ID, who seek to declaw it by denying that it is, at heart, a scientific revolution. According to its most acerbic adversaries, ID is merely a religious ruse wearing a scientific facade. For philosopher Barbara Forrest, "The intelligent design movement as a whole . . . really has nothing to do with science," but is rather "religious to its core . . . merely the newest 'evolution' of good old-fashioned American creationism." Zoologists Matthew Brauer and Daniel Brumbaugh charge that the ID movement "is not motivated by new scientific discoveries" but "entirely by the religion and politics of a small group of academics who seek to defeat secular 'modernist naturalism' by updating previously discredited creationist approaches." The most outspoken critic of ID theory, philosopher Robert Pennock (who has published two anti-ID books), likewise asserts in *Intelligent Design Creationism and Its Critics* that ID is merely a "theological movement" with a "game plan . . . little different than that of the 'creation scientists'" and suspects that at the heart of the ID urge is a regrettable and benighted "tendency to anthropomorphize the world," to see design in nature only because we are designers ourselves.

As should be clear from the incessant cry of alarm—"Creationist! Creationist!"—the source of the critics' ire is that ID has dared to enter the realm of biology and raise questions concerning the near sacrosanct canons of Darwinism. (And if one starts questioning the Darwinian account of man's origin and nature, what aspect of our secularized culture could escape uprooting?) 'Tis all fine and good, they say, to investigate cosmological fine-tuning but anathema to consider biological fine-tuning. Indeed, such critics seem to think that doubting evolutionary theory's claims to have eliminated design from biology could only occur if one has either lost one's mind or placed it on an out-of-the-way shelf marked "Do Not Disturb" (the embarassing result of irrational adherence to an entirely mytho-theological account of creation). They seem—to get to the bottom of it—to agree with the words of zoologist and evolutionary spokesman laureate Richard Dawkins: "It is absolutely safe to say that if you meet someone who claims not to believe in evolution, that person is ignorant, stupid or insane (or wicked, but I'd rather not consider that)."

> *ID has dared to enter the realm of biology and raise questions concerning the near sacrosanct canons of Darwinism.*

Against this, I argue not only that it is quite reasonable to have doubts about evolutionary theory, but that the rise and development of ID theory, as an antidote to Darwinism, is both intellectually welcome and historically inevitable. It is intellectually welcome because Darwinism is too small to fit the facts it claims to explain, and ID is large enough to include a modified form of Darwinism. . . .

What ID Accepts from Darwin

What then are the most significant defects in Darwinism? Not that it has provided an account of descent with modification— that's one of its merits—but that its proposed mechanisms allowing it to eliminate intelligence as a cause are woefully insufficient. To understand this, let's return to the cosmological level.

ID theory affirms the universe to be 15 billion years old (more or less) and endorses the generally accepted account of the wonderful unfolding of stellar and planetary evolution. But it makes clear that it is the original and inherent fine-tuning that allows the unfolding to occur. ID proponents look at the wonderful and wonderfully strange history of life the same way. They do not deny many of the marvelous things that Darwinism has uncovered, and so an ID account of biology would include much of what Darwinists have discovered. What they question, however, is the Darwinian insertion that such things are explicable solely as the result of purposeless, unguided mechanisms. . . .

> *Has everything unfolded smoothly according to the assumptions, or has Darwinism found its critical assumptions ramming into stubborn . . . facts?*

If the elimination of design in biology was wrongheaded, then the mechanism by which Darwin tried to exclude it must somehow be faulty or incomplete. To that mechanism we must now turn.

The initial evidence for design-free evolution provided by Darwin is powerful, especially if one understands the particular context of belief reigning at the time of Darwin. The common belief about species at the time was that God created all the stunning varieties of plants and animals as they now appeared (and did so, a mere 6,000 years prior). Darwin effectively demolished this particular belief in the Origin by beginning with incontrovertible evidence of the malleability [the ability to be changed] of species right under the English nose. After all, he noted, we must admit that breeders of animals, through the artifice of selecting for desired traits and breeding to exaggerate them, are able to produce, in comparatively few generations, radically different looking stock. Obviously, these very different breeds were created by man and did not come, ready-made, from the hand of God.

From the example of the plasticity of breeds under domestication, Darwin then asked: "Can the principle of selection, which we have seen is so potent in the hands of man, apply under nature?" How could it not? the reader asks himself. "Can it, then, be thought improbable," Darwin mused, that "variations useful in some way to each being in the great and complex battle of life, should occur in the course of many successive generations? If such do occur, can we doubt (remembering that many more individuals are born than can possibly survive) that individuals having any advantage, however slight, over others, would have the best chance of surviving and of procreating their kind?" Yes, of course, the reader concludes, natural selection, the source of the endless varieties we find within natural species—innumerable varieties of sparrows, oodles of turtles, countless variations of snakes!

A brilliant step forward in the history of science, for which we owe Darwin a great debt. Had he stopped there, Darwin would have successfully defeated the particular belief that God had immediately created every variety of plant and animal. Of course, that small victory could not, by itself, establish the larger claim that biology was designer-free. In order to eliminate a designer completely Darwin had to make the great inferential leap from partial, legitimate insight to an all-encompassing theory, from change within limits, to unlimited change: "Slow though the process of selection may be," Darwin intoned, "if feeble man can do much by artificial selection, I can see no limit to the amount of change . . . which may have been effected in the long course of time through nature's power of selection, that is by the survival of the fittest." Small changes add up to distinct varieties; with time, the varietal branches become more distinct until they rank as species; with yet more time, the changes become so pronounced that we class them as being in distinct genera, and so on, until voilà, we have the famous evolutionary tree.

What ID Rejects

The test of this great leap is, of course, whether or not what it predicts, according to its assumptions, pans out if we study nature . . . for a sufficient length of time. Has everything unfolded smoothly according to the assumptions, or has Darwinism found its critical assumptions ramming into stubborn . . . facts?

Where has Darwinism succeeded grandly? Exactly where it succeeded at first, in describing relatively small-scale evolution, often called microevolution. So where has it failed? In those precise places where it would need to have succeeded in order to make good on the great daring inference. We will look at two: (1) the need for a gradual appearance of the highest biological taxa [taxanomic group] and (2) the extension of design-free biology backwards to a gradual nondirected rise of the first cells from prebiological materials. Both of these are necessary to exclude ID from biology.

> // *The sudden appearance of nearly all modern biological phyla completely contradicts the expectations of Darwin's theory.* //

The sharpest rocks to dash the expectations of Darwinism were quarried in Canada at the beginning of the 20th century, and the fossils taken from this wonderful site, called the Burgess Shale, lay entirely misinterpreted for almost three-quarters of a century. They provide us with a most illuminating window into the Cambrian explosion, where, in evolutionist Stephen Jay Gould's words, "in a geological moment near the beginning of the Cambrian [about 570 million years ago], nearly all modern phyla made their first appearance, along with an even greater array of anatomical experiments that did not survive very long thereafter." This appearance is not the result of a gradual rise (through innumerable intermediate species) of increasingly more complex life leading up to the Cambrian period. Rather, in Gould's words, it occurs "with a bang" in a "geological flash" as a "gigantic burp of creativity."

Why is the Cambrian such a stick in the craw of Darwinism? Darwin's principle *natura non facit saltum* (nature does not make a leap) is the principle by which evolutionary theory can eliminate intelligence as a cause. How so? Intelligence, as a cause, can create elaborate order quickly and efficiently: *ratio facit salta* (reason does make leaps), we might well say. If the unintelligent meanderings of natural selection are to displace an Intelligent Designer, then, as Darwin realized, all big differences must be the result of the addition of countless very little differences. The sudden appearance of nearly all modern biological phyla completely contradicts the expectations of Darwin's theory. The taxonomic hierarchy in biology, from greatest difference to least, is kingdom, phylum, class, order, family, genus, and species. As

Darwin well understood, the greater the difference, the greater the number of transitional species required, and the greater amount of time natural selection will need, working through slight variations, to produce the far greater differences characteristic of phyla. For Darwin, phyla simply cannot appear abruptly but must be the result of a long, arduous, winding path of slight variations among a discrete population leading, by natural selection, to new varieties, which in turn, lead to new species, which in turn . . . and so on, until one reaches the level of divergence indicative of phyla. If Darwin were right, the fossil evidence would support him.

> *There are [insurmountable] problems in trying to explain, via some mode of design-free evolutionary theory, how the first cells could have arisen.*

The sudden appearance of all known phyla in the Cambrian, therefore, represents a first-order theoretical crisis for Darwinism. For an ID approach, it indicates the presence of causal intelligence. While nature itself *non facit saltum*, such leaps are the hallmark of a designing intellect, especially since the phyla level acts as a kind of plan allowing for future evolutionary development (in a somewhat analogous way that fine-tuning of physical constants allows for stellar evolution).

Does that prove that ID theory has won in biology by default? No. It only proves that (1) it is reasonable to doubt that natural selection, powerful as it may be in certain domains, can displace intelligence as a cause in the origin of animal design, and more particularly, (2) it is reasonable to investigate the fossil evidence from the perspective of design. . . .

Evolution and the Origin of Life

There are insuperable [insurmountable] problems in trying to explain, via some mode of design-free evolutionary theory, how the first cells could have arisen. Nobel laureate biochemist Francis Crick, codiscoverer of the helical structure of DNA, has even remarked, "An honest man, armed with all the knowledge available to us now, could only state that in some sense, the origin of life appears at the moment to be almost a miracle, so many are the conditions which would have had to have been satisfied to get it going." The enigma drove Crick to offer a nonevolutionary solution to the origin of life, the theory of panspermia, the belief that intelligent aliens seeded life on earth.

> // *One would have to be insanely wedded to materialism and have more faith in the powers of chance than any theist has in the powers of God to believe an actual waving statue was not a miracle.* //

Others, such as Dawkins, lapse into an irrational faith in the powers of chance to avoid an ID inference. While Dawkins agrees with Crick that the origin of life is a miracle, by that he means a miracle of chance. But Dawkins believes that anything can be explained by chance, even a miracle. Speaking of a marble statue, Dawkins (with a straight face) argues that "if, by sheer coincidence, all the molecules [in the hand of the statue] just happened to move in the same direction at the same moment, the hand would move. If they then all reversed direction at the same moment the hand would move back. In this way it is possible for a marble statue to wave at us. It could happen."

Of course, one would have to be insanely wedded to materialism and have more faith in the powers of chance than any theist has in the powers of God to believe an actual waving statue was not a miracle. With this faith in the random jostling of molecules, Dawkins sees no trouble in believing (even without evidence) that a materialist miracle occurred, albeit he knows not how, allowing for the rise of the first living cells. Such faith, however, is not evidence itself but a telling lapse into a materialist *credo quia absurdum est.*

The Future of ID

I have spent quite a few words trying to show that the ID movement is both larger than its well-publicized and strongly criticized attempts to question Darwinism and also that it is justified in publicly and strongly criticizing Darwinism. I believe that this analysis allows us to see the merit of the work done so far by ID proponents Michael Behe and William Dembski. Behe's wonderful arguments about the irreducible complexity of biological structures (*Darwin's Black Box*) show clearly that biological fine-tuning is a real problem for Darwinism precisely because of the discovery of the unfathomable complexity of even the smallest biological structures. Dembski (most recently, *No Free Lunch*) has declared war, so to speak, on the kind of irrational reliance on chance all too characteristic of Darwinism and seen all too clearly in Dawkins. Such reliance, we recall, is rooted in the desire to eliminate the design inference in biology, and Dembski's arguments are essential to removing such irrational obstacles.

Where is the ID revolution headed? Time will tell. But it's a young movement, after all. As with all scientific and philosophical revolutions—so also with ID—one is not able to predict what this mode of scientific inquiry will discover.

3

Molecules Were Designed by a Creator

Michael Behe

Michael Behe is professor of biological sciences at Lehigh University in Bethlehem, Pennsylvania. He is the author of Darwin's Black Box: The Biochemical Challenge to Evolution.

In *Origin of Species*, Darwin wrote that if it can be proved that any organ exists that "could not possibly have been formed by numerous, successive, slight modifications, [his] theory [of evolution] would absolutely break down." A system that fits this criterion is one that is irreducibly complex, such as that of the bacterial flagellum. Irreducibly complex systems could not have evolved through numerous, successive, slight modifications because if any one part is changed or taken away, the whole system fails. A more compelling explanation for their existence is that they were designed by an intelligent designer. Some critics have tried to falsify irreducible complexity and Intelligent Design, but a closer look at the examples they use actually supports Intelligent Design. For example, Kenneth Miller asserts that experiments done on a lactose-utilizing system in E. coli prove that the system could have evolved. In fact, though, the experiments were only successful after significant intelligent intervention, which is in line with the expectations of irreducible complexity and highlights the limits of Darwinism.

Michael Behe, "The Modern Intelligent Design Hypothesis: Breaking the Rules," *Philosophia Christi*, vol. 3, 2001. Copyright © 2001 by *Philosophia Christi*. Reproduced by permission.

I n 1859 Charles Darwin published his great work *On the Origin of Species*, in which he proposed to explain how the great variety and complexity of the natural world might have been produced solely by the action of blind physical processes. His proposed mechanism was, of course, natural selection working on random variation. In a nutshell, Darwin reasoned that the members of a species whose chance variation gave them an edge in the struggle to survive would tend to survive and reproduce. If the variation could be inherited, then over time the characteristics of the species would change. And over great periods of time, perhaps great changes would occur.

It was a very elegant idea. Nonetheless, Darwin knew his proposed mechanism could not explain everything, and in *Origin* he gave us a criterion by which to judge his theory. He wrote:

> If it could be demonstrated that any complex organ existed which could not possibly have been formed by numerous, successive, slight modifications, my theory would absolutely break down.

Irreducibly Complex

He added, however, that he could "find out no such case." Darwin of course was justifiably interested in protecting his fledgling theory from easy dismissal, and so he threw the burden of proof—to prove a negative, to "demonstrate" that something "could not possibly" have happened—onto his opponents, which is essentially impossible to do in science. Nonetheless, let's ask what might at least potentially meet Darwin's criterion? What sort of organ or system seems unlikely to be formed by "numerous successive, slight modifications"? A good place to start is with one that is irreducibly complex. In *Darwin's Black Box: The Biochemical Challenge to Evolution,* I defined an irreducibly complex system as:

> [A] single system which is composed of several well-matched, interacting parts that contribute to the basic function, and where the removal of any one of the parts causes the system to effectively cease functioning.

A good illustration of an irreducibly complex system from our everyday world is a simple mechanical mousetrap. A common mousetrap has several parts, including a wooden platform, a spring with extended ends, a hammer, holding bar, and catch. Now, if the mousetrap is missing the spring, or hammer, or platform, it doesn't catch mice half as well as it used to, or a quarter as well. It simply doesn't catch mice at all. Therefore it is irreducibly complex. It turns out that irreducibly complex systems are headaches for Darwinian theory, because they are resistant to being produced in the gradual, step-by-step manner that Darwin envisioned.

> *What sort of organ or system seems unlikely to be formed by 'numerous successive, slight modifications'? A good place to start is with one that is irreducibly complex.*

As biology has progressed with dazzling speed in the past half-century, we have discovered many systems in the cell, at the very foundation of life, which, like a mousetrap, are irreducibly complex. Time permits me to mention only one example here—the bacterial flagellum. The flagellum is quite literally an outboard motor that some bacteria use to swim. It is a rotary device that, like a boat's motor, turns a propeller to push against liquid, moving the bacterium forwards in the process. It consists of a number of parts, including a long tail that acts as a propeller, the hook region that attaches the propeller to the drive shaft, the motor that uses a flow of acid from the outside of the bacterium to the inside to power the turning, a stator that keeps the structure stationary in the plane of the membrane while the propeller turns, and bushing material to allow the drive shaft to poke up through the bacterial membrane. In the absence of the hook, or the motor, or the propeller, or the drive shaft, or most of the forty different types of proteins that genetic studies have shown to be necessary for the activity or construction of the flagellum, one doesn't get a flagellum that spins half as fast as it used to, or a quarter as fast. Either the flagellum doesn't work, or it doesn't even get constructed in the cell. Like a mousetrap, the flagellum is irreducibly complex. And again, like the mousetrap, its evolutionary development by "numerous, successive, slight modifications" is quite difficult to envision. In fact, if one examines the scientific literature, one quickly sees that no one has ever proposed a serious detailed model for how the flagel-

lum might have arisen in a Darwinian manner, let alone conducted experiments to test such a model. Thus in a flagellum we
seem to have a serious candidate to meet Darwin's criterion. We
have a system that seems very unlikely to have been produced
by "numerous, successive, slight modifications.". . .

> *// No one has ever proposed a serious, detailed model for how the flagellum might have arisen in a Darwinian manner. //*

In *Darwin's Black Box*, I proposed that, rather than Darwinian evolution a more compelling explanation for the irreducibly complex molecular machines discovered in the cell is
that they were indeed designed. . . .

Although I think that ID [Intelligent Design] is a rather obvious hypothesis, nonetheless my book seems to have caught a
number of people by surprise, and so it has been reviewed
pretty widely. The *New York Times*, the *Washington Post*, the *Al-
lentown Morning Call*—all the major media have taken a look at
it. Unexpectedly, not everyone agreed with me. In fact, in response to my argument, several scientists have pointed to experimental results that, they claim, either cast much doubt
over the claim of ID, or falsify it outright. In the remainder of
the [viewpoint] I will discuss these counter-examples. I hope to
show why I think they not only fail to support Darwinism, but
why they actually fit much better with a theory of ID. After
that, I will discuss the issue of falsifiability.

Kenneth Miller's Counter-Example

Kenneth Miller, a professor of cell biology at Brown University,
has written a book recently, entitled *Finding Darwin's God*, in
which he defends Darwinism from a variety of critics, including myself. In a chapter devoted to rebutting *Darwin's Black
Box*, he quite correctly states that "a true acid test" of the ability of Darwinism to deal with irreducible complexity would be
to "[use] the tools of molecular genetics to wipe out an existing
multipart system and then see if evolution can come to the res-
cue with a system to replace it." He then cites the careful work
over the past twenty-five years of Barry Hall of the University of

Rochester on the experimental evolution of a lactose-utilizing system in *E. coli*.

Here is a brief description of how the system, called the *lac* operon, functions. The *lac* operon of *E. coli* contains genes coding for several proteins that are involved in the metabolism of a type of sugar called lactose. One protein of the *lac* operon, called a permease, imports lactose through the otherwise impermeable cell membrane. Another protein is an enzyme called galactosidase, which can break down lactose to its two constituent monosaccharides, galactose and glucose, which the cell can then process further. Because lactose is rarely available in the environment, the bacterial cell switches off the genes until lactose is available. The switch is controlled by another protein called a repressor, whose gene is located next to the operon. Ordinarily the repressor binds to the *lac* operon, shutting it off by physically interfering with the operon. However, in the presence of the natural "inducer" allolactose or the artificial chemical inducer IPTG, the repressor binds to the inducer and releases the operon, allowing the *lac* operon enzymes to be synthesized by the cell. . . .

> *Rather than Darwinian evolution a more compelling explanation for the irreducibly complex molecular machines discovered in the cell is that they were indeed designed.*

The prose in Miller's book obscures the facts that most of the lactose system was already in place when the experiments began, that the system was carried through non-viable states by inclusion of IPTG, and that the system will not function without pre-existing components. From a skeptical perspective, the admirably careful work of Barry Hall involved a series of micromutations stitched together by intelligent intervention. He showed that the activity of a deleted enzyme could be replaced only by mutations to a second, homologous protein with a nearly identical active site; and only if the second repressor already bound lactose; and only if the system were also artificially induced by IPTG: and only if the system were also allowed to use a pre-existing permease. In my view, such results are entirely in line with the expectations of irreducible complexity requiring intelligent intervention, and of limited capabilities for Darwinian processes.

Russell Doolittle's Counter-Example

A second putative counter-example to ID concerns the blood-clotting system. Blood clotting is a very intricate biochemical process, requiring many protein parts. I had devoted a chapter of *Darwin's Black Box* to the blood-clotting cascade, claiming that it is irreducibly complex and so does not fit well within a Darwinian framework. However, Russell Doolittle, a prominent biochemist, member of the National Academy of Sciences, and expert on blood clotting, disagreed. . . .

> *Such results are entirely in line with the expectations of irreducible complexity requiring intelligent intervention, and of limited capabilities for Darwinian processes.*

Doolittle cited a paper by [T.H.] Bugge *et al.* entitled "Loss of fibrinogen rescues mice from the pleiotropic effects of plasminogen deficiency." (By way of explanation, fibrinogen is the precursor of the clot material; plasminogen is a protein that degrades blood clots.) He commented:

> Recently the gene for plaminogen [*sic*] was knocked out of mice, and, predictably, those mice had thrombotic complications because fibrin clots could not be cleared away. Not long after that, the same workers knocked out the gene for fibrinogen in another line of mice. Again, predictably, these mice were ailing, although in this case hemorrhage was the problem. And what do you think happened when these two lines of mice were crossed? For all practical purposes, the mice lacking both genes were normal! Contrary to claims about irreducible complexity, the entire ensemble of proteins is not needed. Music and harmony can arise from a smaller orchestra.

The implied argument seems to be that the modern clotting system is actually not irreducibly complex, and so a simpler clotting cascade might be missing factors such as plasminogen and fibrinogen, and perhaps it could be expanded into the modern clotting system by gene duplication. However, that interpretation does not stand up to a careful reading of Bugge *et al.*

In their paper, Bugge *et al.* note that the lack of plasminogen in mice results in many problems, such as high mortality, ulcers, severe thrombosis, and delayed wound healing. On the other hand, lack of fibrinogen results in failure to clot, frequent hemorrhage, and death of females during pregnancy. The point of Bugge *et al.* was that if one crosses the two knockout strains, producing plasminogen-plus-fibrinogen deficiency in individual mice, the mice do not suffer the many problems that afflict mice lacking plasminogen alone. Since the title of the paper emphasized that mice were "rescued" from some ill effects, one might be misled into thinking that the double-knockout mice were normal. They are not. As Bugge *et al.* state in their abstract, "Mice deficient in plasminogen and fibrinogen are phenotypically indistinguishable from fibrinogen-deficient mice." In other words, the double-knockouts have all the problems that mice lacking only fibrinogen have: they do not form clots, they hemorrhage, and the females die if they become pregnant. They are definitely not promising evolutionary intermediates. . . .

> *One can't say both that ID is unfalsifiable (or untestable) and that there is evidence against it.*

The double-knockout mice do not merely have a less sophisticated but still functional clotting system. They have no functional clotting system at all. They are not evidence for the Darwinian evolution of blood clotting. Therefore my argument, that the system is irreducibly complex, is unaffected by this example. . . .

Falsifiability

Let us now consider the issue of falsifiability. Let me say up front that I know most philosophers of science do not regard falsifiability as a necessary trait of a successful scientific theory.

Nonetheless, falsifiabilty is still an important factor to consider since it is nice to know whether or not one's theory can be shown to be wrong by contact with the real world.

A frequent charge made against ID is that it is unfalsifiable, or untestable. For example, in its recent booklet *Science and Creationism* the National Academy of Sciences writes:

> Intelligent design . . . [is] not science because [it is] not testable by the methods of science.

Yet that claim seems to be at odds with the criticisms I have just summarized. Clearly, both Russell Doolittle and Kenneth Miller advanced scientific arguments aimed at falsifying ID. If the results of Bugge *et al.* had been as Doolittle first thought, or if Barry Hall's work had indeed shown what Miller implied, then they correctly believed that my claims about irreducible complexity would have suffered quite a blow.

> *In the history of science, the scientific community has believed in any number of things that were in fact not true, not real.*

Now, one can't have it both ways. One can't say both that ID is unfalsifiable (or untestable) and that there is evidence against it. Either it is unfalsifiable and floats serenely beyond experimental reproach, or it can be criticized on the basis of our observations and is therefore testable. The fact that critical reviewers advance scientific arguments against ID (whether successfully or not) shows that they think ID is indeed falsifiable. What's more, it is wide open to falsification by a series of rather straightforward laboratory experiments such as those that Miller and Doolittle pointed to, which is exactly why they pointed to them. . . .

It seems then, perhaps counter-intuitively to some, that ID is quite susceptible to falsification, at least on the points under discussion. Darwinism, on the other hand, seems quite impervious to falsification. The reason for this can be seen when we examine the basic claims of the two ideas with regard to a particular biochemical system like, say, the bacterial flagellum. The claim of ID is that "*No* unintelligent process could produce this system." The claim of Darwinism is that "*Some* unintelligent process could produce this system." To falsify the first claim, one need only show that at least one unintelligent process could produce the system. To falsify the second claim, one would have to show the system could not have been formed by any of a potentially infinite number of possible unintelligent processes, which is effectively impossible to do.

The danger of accepting an effectively unfalsifiable hypothesis is that science has no way to determine if the belief corresponds to reality. In the history of science, the scientific community has believed in any number of things that were in fact not true, not real—for example, the universal ether. If there were no way to test those beliefs, the progress of science might be substantially and negatively affected. If, in the present case, the expansive claims of Darwinism are in reality not true, then its unfalsifiability will cause science to bog down in these areas, as I believe it has.

So, what can be done? I don't think that the answer is to never investigate a theory that is unfalsifiable. After all, although it is unfalsifiable, Darwinism's claims are potentially positively demonstrable. For example, if some scientist conducted an experiment showing the production of a flagellum (or some equally complex system) by Darwinian processes, then the Darwinian claim would be affirmed. The question only arises in the face of negative results.

I think several steps can be prescribed. First of all, one has to be aware—raise one's consciousness—about when a theory is unfalsifiable. Second, as far as possible, an advocate of an unfalsifiable theory should try as diligently as possible to demonstrate positively the claims of the hypothesis. Third, one needs to relax Darwin's criterion from this:

> If it could be demonstrated that any complex organ existed which could not possibly have been formed by numerous, successive, slight modifications, my theory would absolutely break down.

to something like this:

> If a complex organ exists which seems very unlikely to have been produced by numerous, successive, slight modifications, and if no experiments have shown that it or comparable structures can be so produced, then maybe we're barking up the wrong tree. So . . .

Let's break some rules!

Of course, people will differ on the point at which they decide to break rules. But at least with the realistic criterion there could be evidence against the unfalsifiable. At least then people like Doolittle and Miller would run a risk when they cite an experiment that shows the opposite of what they had thought. At least then science would have a way to escape from the rut of unfalsifiability and think new thoughts.

4

Molecular Biology Points to Evolution

Kenneth R. Miller

Kenneth R. Miller is a cell biologist and professor of biology at Brown University in Providence, Rhode Island. He has published articles in journals such as Nature, Scientific American, *and* Cell. *He is also the author of the book* Finding Darwin's God: A Scientist's Search for Common Ground Between God and Evolution.

The creationist movement holds up the bacterial flagellum as proof of an intelligent designer. Adherents say the flagellum could not have evolved because it is "irreducibly complex." In other words, when one of the flagellum's parts is taken away, it does not function—and evolution only works on functioning systems. But research has shown that the flagellum evolved from another system, the type III secretory system (TTSS). The TTSS serves a valuable purpose for a wide variety of bacteria, a purpose that is completely separate from the flagellum's purpose. The fact that a small portion of the "irreducibly complex" flagellum can carry out such an important biological function disproves the assertion that the flagellum must be fully assembled before any of its component parts can be useful. The flagellum is clearly not irreducibly complex and fails as proof of an intelligent designer. Instead, it proves evolution.

Almost from the moment *The Origin of Species* was published in 1859, the opponents of evolution have fought a long, losing battle against their Darwinian foes. Today, like a prize-

Kenneth R. Miller, "The Flagellum Unspun: The Collapse of 'Irreducible Complexity,'" *Debating Design: From Darwin to DNA*, edited by William A. Dembski and Michael Ruse. New York: Cambridge University Press, 2004. Copyright © 2004 by Cambridge University Press. Reproduced by permission.

fighter in the late rounds losing badly on points, they've placed their hopes in one big punch—a single claim that might smash through the overwhelming weight of scientific evidence to bring Darwin to the canvas once and for all. Their name for this virtual roundhouse right is "intelligent design."

In the last several years, the intelligent design movement has attempted to move against science education standards in several American states, most famously in Kansas and Ohio. The principal claim made by adherents of this view is that they can detect the presence of "intelligent design" in complex biological systems. As evidence, they cite a number of specific examples, including the vertebrate blood clotting cascade, the eukaryotic cilium, and most notably, the eubacterial flagellum.

Poster Child

Of all these examples, the flagellum has been presented so often as a counter-example to evolution that it might well be considered the "poster child" of the modern anti-evolution movement. Variations of its image now appear on web pages of anti-evolution groups like the Discovery Institute, and on the covers of "intelligent design" books such as William Dembski's *No Free Lunch*. To anti-evolutionists, the high status of the flagellum reflects the supposed fact that it could not possibly have been produced by an evolutionary pathway.

> *There is, to be sure, nothing new or novel in an anti-evolutionist pointing to a complex or intricate natural structure, and professing skepticism that it could have been produced by the 'random' processes of mutation and natural selection.*

There is, to be sure, nothing new or novel in an anti-evolutionist pointing to a complex or intricate natural structure, and professing skepticism that it could have been produced by the "random" processes of mutation and natural selection. Nonetheless, the "argument from personal incredulity," as such sentiment has been appropriately described, has been a weapon of little value in the anti-evolution movement. Anyone can state at any time that *they* cannot imagine how evolutionary mechanisms might have produced a certain species, organ, structure. Such statements, obviously, are personal—and they say more about the limitations of those who make them than they do about the limitations of Darwinian mechanisms.

> **❧ *Why does the intelligent design movement regard the flagellum as unevolvable? Because it is said to possess a quality known as 'irreducible complexity.'* ❧**

The hallmark of the intelligent design movement, however, is that it purports to rise above the level of personal skepticism. It claims to have found a *reason* why evolution could not have produced a structure like the bacterial flagellum, a reason based on sound, solid scientific evidence.

Why does the intelligent design movement regard the flagellum as unevolvable? Because it is said to possess a quality known as "irreducible complexity." Irreducibly complex structures, we are told, could not have been produced by evolution, or, for that matter, by any natural process. They do exist, however, and therefore they must have been produced by something. That something could only be an outside intelligent agency operating beyond the laws of nature—an intelligent designer. That, simply stated, is the core of the new argument from design, and the intellectual basis of the intelligent design movement.

The great irony of the flagellum's increasing acceptance as an icon of anti-evolution is the fact that research had demolished its status as an example of irreducible complexity almost at the very moment it was first proclaimed. The purpose of this article is to explore the arguments by which the flagellum's notoriety has been achieved, and to review the research development that have now undermined the very foundations of those arguments.

The Argument's Origins

The flagellum owes its status principally to *Darwin's Black Box*, a book by Michael Behe that employed it in a carefully crafted anti-evolution argument. Building upon William Paley's well-known "argument from design," Behe sought to bring the argument two centuries forward into the realm of biochemistry. Like Paley, Behe appealed to his readers to appreciate the intricate complexity of living organisms as evidence for the work of a designer. Unlike Paley, however, he raised the argument to a new level, claiming to have discovered a scientific principle that could be used to prove that certain structures could not have been produced by evolution. That principle goes by the name of "irreducible complexity."

> *The lack of a detailed current explanation for a structure, organ, or process does not mean that science will never come up with one.*

An irreducibly complex structure is defined by Behe as ". . . a single system composed of several well-matched, interacting parts that contribute to the basic function, wherein the removal of any one of the parts causes the system to effectively cease functioning." Why would such systems present difficulties for Darwinism? Because they could not possibly have been produced by the process of evolution:

> An irreducibly complex system cannot be produced directly by numerous successive, slight modifications of a precursor system, because any precursor to an irreducibly complex system that is missing a part is by definition nonfunctional. . . . Since natural selection can only choose systems that are already working, then if a biological system cannot be produced gradually it would have to arise as an integrated unit, in one fell swoop, for natural selection to have anything to act on.

The phrase "numerous, successive, slight modification" is not accidental. The very same words were used by Charles Darwin in *The Origin of Species* in describing the conditions that had to be met for his theory to be true. As Darwin wrote, if one could find an organ or structure that could not have been formed by "numerous, successive, slight modifications," his "theory would absolutely break down." To anti-evolutionists, the bacterial flagellum is now regarded as exactly such a case—an "irreducibly complex system" which "cannot be produced directly by numerous successive, slight modifications." A system that could not have evolved—a desperation punch that just might win the fight in the final round—a tool with which the theory of evolution can be brought down.

The Logic of Irreducible Complexity

Living cells are filled, of course, with complex structures whose detailed evolutionary origins are not known. Therefore, in fashioning an argument against evolution one might pick nearly any cellular structure, the ribosome for example, and claim—correctly—that its origin has not been explained in detail by evolution.

Such arguments are easy to make, of course, but the nature of scientific progress renders them far from compelling. The lack of a detailed current explanation for a structure, organ, or process does not mean that science will never come up with one. As an example, one might consider the question of how left-right asymmetry arises in vertebrate development, a question that was beyond explanation until the 1990s. In 1990 one might have argued that the body's left-right asymmetry could just as well be explained by the intervention of a designer as by an unknown molecular mechanism. Only a decade after, the actual molecular mechanism was identified, and any claim one might have made for the intervention of a designer would have been discarded. The same point can be made, of course, regarding any structure or mechanism whose origins are not yet understood.

> **//** *The flagellum is presented as a 'molecular machine' whose individual parts must have been specifically crafted to work as a unified assembly.* **//**

The utility of the bacterial flagellum is that it seems to rise above this "argument from ignorance." By asserting that it is a structure "in which the removal of an element would cause the whole system to cease functioning," the flagellum is presented as a "molecular machine" whose individual parts must have been specifically crafted to work as a unified assembly. The existence of such a multipart machine therefore provides genuine scientific proof of the actions of an intelligent designer.

> **❝** *The existence of the TTSS in a wide variety of bacteria demonstrates that a small portion of the 'irreducibly complex' flagellum can indeed carry out an important biological function.* **❞**

In the case of the flagellum, the assertion of irreducible complexity means that a minimum number of protein components, perhaps 30, are required to produce a working biological function. By the logic of irreducible complexity, these individual components should have no function until all 30 are put into place, at which point the function of motility appears. What this means, of course, is that evolution could not have fashioned those components a few at a time, since they do not have functions that could be favored by natural selection. As Behe wrote: ". . . natural selection can only choose among systems that are already working," and an irreducibly complex system does not work unless all of its parts are in place. The flagellum is irreducibly complex, and therefore, it must have been designed. Case closed.

Answering the Argument

The assertion that cellular machines are irreducibly complex, and therefore provide proof of design, has not gone unnoticed by the scientific community. A number of detailed rebuttals have appeared in the literature, and many have pointed out the poor reasoning of recasting the classic argument from design in the modern language of biochemistry. I have suggested elsewhere that the scientific literature contains counter-examples to any assertion that evolution cannot have biochemical complexity, and other workers have addressed the issue of how evolutionary mechanisms allow biological systems to increase in information content.

The most powerful rebuttals to the flagellum story, however, have not come from direct attempts to answer the critics of evolution. Rather, they have emerged from the steady progress of scientific work on the genes and proteins associated with the flagellum and other cellular structures. Such studies have now established that the entire premise by which this molecular machine has been advanced as an argument against evolution is wrong—the bacterial flagellum is not irreducibly complex. As we will see, the flagellum—the supreme example of the power of this new "science of design"—has failed its most basic scientific test. Remember the claim that "any precursor to an irreducibly complex system that is missing a part is by definition nonfunctional?" As the evidence has shown, nature is filled with examples of "precursors" to the flagellum that are indeed "missing a part," and yet are fully-functional. Functional enough, in some cases, to pose a serious threat to human life.

The Type III Secretory Apparatus

In the popular imagination, bacteria are "germs"—tiny microscopic bugs that make us sick. Microbiologists smile at that generalization, knowing that most bacteria are perfectly benign, and many are beneficial—even essential—to human life. Nonetheless, there are indeed bacteria that produce diseases, ranging from the mildly unpleasant to the truly dangerous. Pathogenic, or disease-causing, bacteria threaten the organisms they infect in a variety of ways, one of which is to produce poisons and inject them directly into the cells of the body. Once inside, these toxins break down and destroy the host cells, producing illness, tissue damage, and sometimes even death.

> *If the flagellum contains within it a smaller functional set of components . . . then the flagellum itself cannot be irreducibly complex—by definition.*

In order to carry out this diabolical work, bacteria must not only produce the protein toxins that bring about the demise of their hosts, but they must efficiently inject them across the cell membranes and into the cells of their hosts. They do this by means of any number of specialized protein secretory systems. One, known as the type III secretory system (TTSS), allows gram negative bacteria to translocate proteins directly into the cytoplasm of a host cell. The proteins transferred through the TTSS include a variety of truly dangerous molecules, some which are known as "virulence factors," and are directly responsible for the pathogenic activity of some of the most deadly bacteria in existence.

> *// Where intelligent design theories throw up their hands and declare defeat for evolution, however, these researchers decided to do the hard scientific work. //*

At first glance, the existence of the TTSS, a nasty little device that allows bacteria to inject these toxins through the cell membranes of its unsuspecting hosts, would seem to have little to do with the flagellum. However, molecular studies of proteins in the TTSS have revealed a surprising fact—the proteins of the TTSS are directly homologous to the proteins in the basal portion of the bacterial flagellum. These homologies extend to a cluster of closely associated proteins found in both of these molecular "machines." On the basis of these homologies, the flagellum itself should be regarded as a type III secretory system. Extending such studies with a detailed comparison of the proteins associated with both systems, Japanese biochemist S.I. Aizawa has seconded this suggestion, noting that the two systems "consist of homologous component proteins with common physico-chemical properties." It is now clear, therefore, that a smaller subset of the full complement of proteins in the flagellum makes up the functional transmembrane portion of the TTSS.

Stated directly, the TTSS does its dirty work using a handful of proteins from the base of the flagellum. From the evolutionary point of view, this relationship is hardly surprising. In fact, it's to be expected that the opportunism of evolutionary processes would mix and match proteins to produce new and novel functions. According to the doctrine of irreducible complexity, however, this should not be possible. If the flagellum is indeed irreducibly complex, then removing just one part, let alone 10 or 15, should render what remains "by definition non-fuctional." Yet the TTSS is indeed fully-functional, even though it is missing most of the parts of the flagellum. The TTSS may be bad news for us, but for the bacteria that possess it, it is a truly valuable biochemical machine.

The existence of the TTSS in a wide variety of bacteria demonstrates that a small portion of the "irreducibly complex" flagellum can indeed carry out an important biological function. Since such a function is clearly favored by natural selection, the contention that the flagellum must be fully-assembled before any of its component parts can be useful is obviously incorrect. What this means is that the argument for intelligent design of the flagellum has failed.

Counterattack

Classically, one of the most widely repeated charges made by anti-evolutionists is that the fossil record contains wide "gaps" for which transitional fossils have never been found. Therefore, the intervention of a creative agency, an intelligent designer, must be invoked to account for each gap. Such gaps, of course, have been filled with increasing frequency by paleontologists— the increasingly rich fossil sequences demonstrating the origins of whales are useful examples. Ironically, the response of anti-evolutionists to such discoveries is frequently to claim that things have only gotten worse for evolution. Where previously there had been just one gap, as a result of the transitional fossil, now there are two (one on either side of the newly discovered specimen).

As word of the relationship between the eubacterial flagellum and the TTSS has begun to spread among the "design" community, the first hints of a remarkably similar reaction have emerged. The TTSS only makes problems worse for evolution, according to this response, because now there are two irreducibly complex systems to deal with. The flagellum is still irreducibly complex—but so is the TTSS. But now there are two systems for evolutionists to explain instead of just one.

Unfortunately for this line of argument, the claim that one irreducibly complex system might contain another is self-contradictory. To understand this, we need to remember that the entire point of the design argument, as exemplified by the flagellum, is that only the entire biochemical machine, with all of its parts, is functional. For the intelligent design argument to stand, this must be the case, since it provides the basis for their claim that only the complete flagellum can be favored by natural selection, not any of its component parts.

However, if the flagellum contains within a smaller functional set of components like the TTSS, then the flagellum itself cannot be irreducibly complex—by definition. Since we now know that this is indeed the case, it is obviously true that the flagellum is not irreducibly complex.

Molecular Evolution

When anti-evolutionary arguments featuring the bacterial flagellum rose into prominence, beginning with the 1996 publication of *Darwin's Black Box*, they were predicated upon the assertion that each of the protein components of the flagellum were crafted, in a single act of design, to fit the specific purpose of the flagellum. The flagellum was said to be unevolvable since the entire complex system had to be assembled first in order to produce any selectable biological function. This claim was broadened to include all complex biological systems, and asserted further that science would never find an evolutionary pathway to any of these systems. After all, it hadn't so far, at least according to one of "design's" principal advocates:

> There is no publication in the scientific literature—in prestigious journals, specialty journals, or books—that describes how molecular evolution of any real, complex, biochemical system either did occur or even might have occurred.

As many critics of intelligent design have pointed out, that statement is simply false. Consider, as just one example, the Krebs cycle, an intricate biochemical pathway consisting of nine enzymes and a number of cofactors that occupies center stage in the pathways of cellular metabolism. The Krebs cycle is "real," "complex," and "biochemical." Does it also present a problem for evolution? Apparently yes, according to the authors of a 1996 paper in the *Journal of Molecular Evolution*, who wrote:

> The Krebs cycle has been frequently quoted as a key problem in the evolution of living cells, hard to explain by Darwin's natural selection: How could natural selection explain the building of a complicated structure in toto, when the intermediate stages have no obvious fitness functionality?

Where intelligent design theorists throw up their hands and

declare defeat for evolution, however, these researchers decided to do the hard scientific work of analyzing the components of the cycle, and seeing if any of them might have been selected for other biochemical tasks. What they found should be a lesson to anyone who asserts that evolution can only act by direct selection for a final function. In fact, nearly all of the proteins of the complex cycle can serve different biochemical purposes within the cell, making it possible to explain in detail how they evolved:

> In the Krebs cycle problem the intermediary stages were also useful, but for different purposes, and, therefore, its complete design was a very clear case of opportunism. . . . The Krebs cycle was built through the process that Jacob (1977) called "evolution by molecular tinkering," stating that evolution does not produce novelties from scratch: It works on what already exists. The most novel result of our analysis is seeing how, with minimal new material, evolution created the most important pathway of metabolism, achieving the best chemically possible design. In this case, a chemical engineer who was looking for the best design of the process could not have found a better design than the cycle which works in living cells.

Since this paper appeared, a 1999 study based on genomic DNA sequences has confirmed the validity of this approach. . . .

> // *A scientific idea rises or falls on the weight of the evidence, and the evidence in the case of the bacterial flagellum is abundantly clear.* //

It is no secret that concepts like "irreducible complexity" and "intelligent design" have failed to take the scientific community by storm. Design has not prompted new research studies, new breakthroughs, or novel insights on so much as a single scientific question. Design advocates acknowledge this from time to time, but they often claim that this is because the scientific deck is stacked against them. The Darwinist establishment, they say, prevents them from getting a foot in the laboratory door.

I would suggest that the real reason for the cold shoulder given "design" by the scientific community, particularly by life science researchers, is because time and time again its principal scientific claims have turned out to be wrong. Science is a pragmatic activity, and if your hypothesis doesn't work, it is quickly discarded.

The Flagellum Unspun

In any discussion of the question of "intelligent design," it is absolutely essential to determine what is meant by the term itself. If, for example, the advocates of design wish to suggest that the intricacies of nature, life, and the universe reveal a world meaning and purpose consistent with an overarching, possibly Divine intelligence, then their point is philosophical, not scientific. It is a philosophical point of view, incidentally, that I share, along with many scientists. As American biologist H. Allen Orr pointed out in a recent review:

> Plenty of scientists have, after all, been attracted to the notion that natural laws reflect (in some way that's necessarily poorly articulated) an intelligence or aesthetic sensibility. This is the religion of Einstein, who spoke of "the grandeur of reason incarnate in existence" and of the scientist's "religious feeling [that] takes the form of a rapturous amazement at the harmony of natural law."

This, however, is not what is meant by "intelligent design" in the parlance of the new anti-evolutionists. Their views demand not a universe in which the beauty and harmony of natural law has brought a world of vibrant and fruitful life into existence, but rather a universe in which the emergence and evolution of life is made expressly impossible by the very same rules. Their view requires that the source of each and every novelty of life was the direct and active involvement of an outside designer whose work violated the very laws of nature he had fashioned. The world of intelligent design is not the bright and innovative world of life that we have come to know through science. Rather, it is a brittle and unchanging landscape, frozen in form and unable to adapt except at the whims of its designer.

Certainly, the issue of design and purpose in nature is a philosophical one that scientists can and should discuss with great vigor. However, the notion at the heart of today's intelligent design movement is that the direct intervention of an outside designer can be demonstrated by the very existence of complex biochemical systems. What even they acknowledge is that their entire scientific position upon a single assertion—that the living cell contains biochemical machines that are irreducibly complex. And the bacterial flagellum is the prime example of such a machine.

> *As Darwin wrote, there is grandeur in an evolutionary view of life, a grandeur that is there for all to see, regardless of their philosophical views on the meaning and purpose of life.*

Such an assertion, as we have seen, can be put to the test in a very direct way. If we are able to search and find an example of a machine with fewer protein parts, contained within the flagellum, that serves a purpose distinct from motility, the claim of irreducible complexity is refuted. As we have also seen, the flagellum does indeed contain such a machine, a protein-secreting apparatus that carries out an important function even in species that lack the flagellum altogether. A scientific idea rises or falls on the weight of the evidence, and the evidence in the case of the bacterial flagellum is abundantly clear.

As an icon of anti-evolution, the flagellum has fallen.

Wonder and Awe Not Diminished

The very existence of the type III secretory system shows that the bacterial flagellum is not irreducibly complex. It also demonstrates, more generally, that the claim of "irreducible complexity" is scientifically meaningless, constructed as it is upon the flimsiest of foundations—the assertion that because science has not yet found selectable functions for the components of a certain structure, it never will. In the final analysis, as the claims of intelligent design fall by the wayside, its advocates are left with a single, remaining tool with which to battle against the rising tide of scientific evidence. That tool may be effective in some circles, of course, but the scientific community will be quick to recognize it for what it really is—the classic argument from ignorance, dressed up in the shiny cloth of biochemistry and information theory.

When three leading advocates of intelligent design were recently given a chance to make their case in an issue of *Natural History* magazine, they each concluded their articles with a plea for design. One wrote that we should recognize "the design inherent in life and the universe," another that "design remains a possibility," and another "that the natural sciences need to leave room for design." Yes, it is true. Design does remain a possibility, but not a type of "intelligent design" of which they speak.

As Darwin wrote, there is a grandeur in an evolutionary view of life, a grandeur that is there for all to see, regardless of their philosophical views on the meaning and purpose of life. I do not believe, even for an instant, that Darwin's vision has weakened or diminished the sense of wonder and awe that one should feel in confronting the magnificence and diversity of the living world. Rather, to a person of faith it should enhance their sense of the Creator's majesty and wisdom. Against such a backdrop, the struggles of the intelligent design movement are best understood as clamorous and disappointing double failures—rejected by science because they do not fit the facts, and having failed religion because they think too little of God.

5

Public Schools Should Teach the Creationism-Evolution Controversy

Francis J. Beckwith

Francis J. Beckwith is Madison Research Fellow in Constitutional Studies and Political Thought at Princeton University. He is also a fellow at the Center for Science and Culture at the Discovery Institute in Seattle and a research fellow at the Newport Institute for Ethics, Law, and Public Policy.

Because religion in the United States has grown more diverse over the years, U.S. courts have established a broad definition of what religion is. The courts have provided guidelines with which to determine if practices and beliefs constitute a religion. According to those guidelines, Intelligent Design (ID) is not a religion. It is a point of view and a scientific research program, the purpose of which is to answer questions about the origin of life on Earth. It is not a religion such as Christianity or Judaism because it does not pass the parallel position test (PPT)— that is, it does not function in the life of the individual in a way parallel to the way in which conventional religion functions in the life of the believer. Therefore, teaching ID in public schools would not violate the establishment clause of the U.S. Constitution, which holds that government can make no laws with regards to the establishment of religion. In modern society, which has different and competing religious and philosophical points of view, a fair evaluation of the question of origins

Francis J. Beckwith, *Law, Darwinism, and Public Education*. Lanham, MD: Rowman & Littlefield, 2003. Copyright © 2003 by Rowman & Littlefield Publishers, Inc. All rights reserved. Reproduced by permission.

must allow the teaching of creationist theory such as ID as well as evolution.

Throughout the history of our republic courts have proposed or implied different definitions of religion, broadening their definitions as the country increased in religious diversity and the judiciary began to face new types of cases. Since the literature on "defining religion" constitutionally is vast, it is not possible to conduct a thorough study in this [viewpoint]. For this reason, I focus on a few important cases and theoretical insights that I believe will be helpful in assessing ID [Intelligent Design].

> **//** *Judge Augustus Hand . . . denied that belief in God was a necessary condition of 'religious training and belief.'* **//**

Although it is true that "the Supreme Court has been reluctant to elaborate an authoritative definition of religion, it has addressed the issue in a number of cases stretching back to the nineteenth century." Religion was defined in early decisions "as an organized body of believers employing religious ceremony and having a faith in and commitment to a supernatural Supreme Being." In an 1890 case, *Davis v. Beason*, the Supreme Court first attempted to give content to the constitutional meaning of religion: "The term 'religion' has reference to one's view of his relations to his Creator, and to the obligations they impose of reverence for his being and character, and of obedience to his will."

Broader Definition of Religion

The modern trend in the courts toward a broader and more global view of religion began in a Second Circuit Court case. The court denied an atheist [a person who denies the existence of God] status as a conscientious objector because his refusal to serve in the military was based exclusively on political grounds. However, in writing for the court, Judge Augustus Hand . . . denied that belief in God was a necessary condition of "religious training and belief" under the congressional statute in question. That is to say, he held that conscientious objection prodded by conscience and grounded in firmly held beliefs that are not conventionally religious could nonetheless be considered "religious," even though Hand believed "it is unnecessary to attempt a definition of religion; the content of the term is found in the history of the human race and is incapable of compression into a few words.". . .

The courts continued to broaden their definition of religion, accepting as religious many belief systems and practices that may not initially strike one as religious. For instance, in *Torcaso v. Watkins* the Supreme Court held that it was unconstitutional for the commonwealth of Maryland to make belief in God a requirement for becoming a notary public. The Court affirmed that a belief system can be religious without being theistic [based on a belief in a god]. "Among religions in this country which do not teach what would generally be considered a belief in God are Buddhism, Taoism, Ethical Culture, Secular Humanism and others." In *United States v. Seeger* the Court ruled that a belief is religious if it is a "sincere and meaningful belief which occupies in the life of its possessor a place parallel to that filled by" traditional belief in God. . . .

> **❝** *Design theory and naturalistic evolution are two conflicting perspectives about the same subject.* **❞**

This type of reasoning is sometimes called the *parallel position test* (PPT), a type of definition by analogy: does the disputed belief function in the life of the individual in a way parallel to the way in which conventional religion functions in the life of the believer? . . .

In order to better understand how modern courts have come to their conclusions about what constitutes a religion, let us engage in a brief thought experiment by trying to answer the philosophical question "What is a religion?" This question has been given many answers. For instance, some have said that a religion is some sort of belief system that necessarily includes a belief in a god and/or life after death. But, as the courts have come to appreciate, one problem with this definition is that it excludes beliefs, such as Taoism and Theravada Buddhism, that are generally thought of as religions but do not include a belief in God or gods. Other religions do not have a full-fledged belief in life after death, as in the cases of early Greek religion and Unitarianism, though no one doubts that they are religions. There are other belief systems, such as Humanism, whose creeds put forth answers to most of the questions traditional religions try to answer. This is why the Supreme Court has said that forms of nontheism can be religion. . . .

> *Naturalistic evolution lends plausibility and support to some nontheisms and thus addresses the same questions as ID but provides different answers.*

In sum, one thing is clear about the courts and religion: they have provided us with no clear definition of religion. Nevertheless, they have provided us with some general guidelines that we can extract from the above analysis:

Conventional religions—e.g., Christianity, Judaism, Buddhism—are paradigm cases of religion.

Whether other belief systems are religious ought to be evaluated by the parallel position test (PPT): Does the disputed belief function in the life of the individual in a way parallel to the way in which conventional religion functions in the life of the believer? . . .

Is ID a Religion?

ID is not a conventional religion and thus is not a paradigm case of a religion. Rather, it is a point of view based on philosophical and empirical arguments. The purpose of ID is to provide answers to the same questions for which the evolutionary paradigm is said to provide answers. That is, design theory and naturalistic evolution are two conflicting perspectives about the same subject. Admittedly, if the ID arguments are plausible, they do lend support to the metaphysical claims of some conventional religions such as Christianity, Judaism, and Islam. However, as Justice Powell wrote in his *Edwards* [Federal Court decision telling that it is unconstitutional to require the teaching of creationism alongside evolution] concurrence, "a decision respecting the subject matter to be taught in public schools does not violate the Establishment Clause simply because the material to be taught 'happens to coincide or harmonize with the tenets of some or all religions.'" After all, . . . the Big Bang theory, the most widely accepted theory of the universe's origin, is more consistent with, and lends support to, theism in comparison to other metaphysical rivals such as atheism. Yet, no one is suggesting that the Big Bang theory ought not to be taught in public schools because it has metaphysical implications friendly to theism and may serve as an impetus for some students to abandon naturalism as a worldview. . . . If a point of view is religious because its plausibility lends support to a religion or a religious point of view, then we would have to conclude that naturalistic evolution is as much a religion as ID, for it lends support to some nontheistic and antireligious perspectives recognized as religions by the Court. Perhaps this is why atheist and skeptic groups are the most vociferous opponents of ID, for they see ID as a possible defeater to evolution, a viewpoint whose truth is essential to the veracity of their worldview, philosophical naturalism.

> // *ID is not 'comprehensive in nature' and it is not a 'belief-system.'* //

Thus, forbidding the teaching of ID (or legitimate criticisms of evolution) in public schools because it lends support to a religion, while exclusively permitting or requiring the teaching of naturalistic evolution unconditionally, might be construed by a court as viewpoint discrimination, a violation of state neutrality on matters of religion, and/or the institutionalizing of a metaphysical orthodoxy, for ID and naturalistic evolution are *not* two different subjects (the first religion, the second science) but two different answers about the same subject. . . .

Applying the Parallel Position Test to ID

Because ID is not a conventional religion, could someone challenge the teaching of it in public schools . . . and legitimately argue that it is a "religion" on the basis of the parallel position test (PPT)? Does ID function in the life of its proponents in a way parallel to the way in which conventional religion functions in the life of the believer? In order to assess whether a purported belief is constitutionally a religion, the Ninth Circuit developed a tripartite application of PPT, which it extracted from prior opinions in the Third Circuit:

> First, a religion addresses fundamental and ultimate questions having to do with deep and imponderable matters. Second, a religion is comprehensive in nature: it consists of a belief-system as opposed to an isolated teaching. Third, a religion often can be recognized by the presence of certain formal and external signs.

(1) ID does not "address fundamental and ultimate questions having to do with deep and imponderable matters." Rather, it addresses the same question raised by Darwinists: What is the origin of apparent design in biological organisms and/or other aspects of the natural universe? Of course, as I pointed out above, design theory lends plausibility and support to theism, but that is not enough for it to meet this test. For naturalistic evolution lends plausibility and support to some nontheisms and thus addresses the same questions as ID but provides different answers. In other words, if one claims that ID meets this test, then one must claim that naturalistic evolution does as well. In addition, to cite Justice Powell yet again, a public school curriculum "does not violate the Establishment Clause simply because the material to be taught 'happens to coincide or harmonize with the tenets of some or all religions.'" Federal Court interference with the policy decisions of local and state educational authorities is warranted "only when the purpose for their decisions is *clearly* religious."

> **❝** One could agree that the courts have consistently held that the concept of God is inherently religious, but that they are simply mistaken. **❞**

(2) ID is not "comprehensive in nature" and it is not a "belief-system." Rather, it is an example of "an isolated teaching," something that is consistent with certain religious belief systems but is itself not a "religion," for one can logically hold

to ID without accepting the comprehensive belief system of any conventional religion. In this sense ID is similar to a moral claim. For example, believing that human beings have intrinsic dignity by nature (a moral claim) is a rationally defensible belief that is consistent with many religious belief systems even though one may logically hold to the position while denying the truth of every religious belief system.

> **//** *ID is a research program whose inferences support, and are consistent with, some belief in a higher intelligence or deity; it is* not *a creed that contains belief in a specific deity as one of its tenets.* **//**

Moreover, design theorists do not defend their position by appealing to esoteric knowledge, special revelation, or religious authority. They make philosophical and scientific arguments whose merits should be assessed by their soundness rather than because their conclusions are inconsistent with philosophical naturalism.

(3) ID does not have the "presence of certain formal and external signs" such as "formal services, ceremonial functions, the existence of clergy, structure and organization, efforts at propagation [increasing the number of its followers] observance of holidays and other similar manifestations associated with traditional religions." Although ID proponents "have formed organizations and institutes, . . . these resemble other academic or professional associations rather than churches or religious institutions."

Thus, according to the general guidelines laid down by the courts, ID is not a religion, and thus to teach it in public schools would not violate the Establishment Clause. . . .

One Final Objection

There is one final objection that one may raise against the teaching of ID in public schools: Because some ID theorists describe the designer in language that is explicitly theological, and others describe it in language that is implicitly theological, and because the courts have said that the concept of God is inherently religious, therefore, even if ID is scientifically sound, the Establishment Clause forbids the teaching of it in public schools.

There are at least three problems with this argument. First, one could agree that the courts have consistently held that the concept of God is inherently religious, but that they are simply mistaken. For the courts ignore the case made by some scholars that "God" need not always be a religious concept, for "God" can be employed as a theoretical postulate without being an object of worship. Since the Supreme Court has shifted and expanded its view of religion over the past 150 years due to America's increasing religious diversity and new insights about the nature of religion, there is no reason why it could not change again. If the Supreme Court in Equal Protection cases can discard opinions on gender because they are anachronistic, it certainly can do the same with outdated definitions of religion.

> *The infusion of Intelligent Design into this debate has changed the legal landscape significantly.*

Second, even if one were to concede that the concept of God is inherently religious, and that the designer in ID is explicitly or implicitly theistic, it does not follow that ID cannot be taught in public schools. . . . ID could be taught for . . . secular reasons [such as to expose students to new scholarship or to maintain neutrality with respect to competing theories], for a religious belief is constitutionally barred from the classroom only if the teaching of it has *no* secular purpose.

Third, it seems reasonable to argue that ID is a research program whose inferences *support*, and are consistent with, some belief in a higher intelligence or deity; it is *not* a creed that contains belief in a specific deity as one of its tenets. . . . To use an analogy, naturalistic evolution is a research program whose inferences *support*, and are consistent with, atheism; it is not a creed that includes unbelief in God as one of its tenets. So, if a scientific research program is "religious" because it supports and is consistent with a belief in a higher intelligence or deity, it would follow that a research program is "irreligious" because it supports and is consistent with the nonexistence of such a being.

In sum, if the concept of God is *not* inherently religious, then ID cannot be barred from public school classrooms for establishment reasons merely because the designer is God; if the concept of God *is* inherently religious, and the designer in ID is implicitly or explicitly theistic, then ID may still be taught in public schools, based on the secular reasons listed above; and if ID is theistic and hence religious because it supports and is consistent with God's existence, then naturalistic evolution is "irreligious" because it supports and is consistent with God's nonexistence, but that would mean that the courts should treat naturalistic evolution like ID. . . .

Not Your Daddy's Fundamentalism

The debate over origins—from *Scopes*[1] to *Edwards* to the present day—is one that touches on some deep and important philosophical and scientific questions about the nature of the universe, knowledge, religion, and liberty. In a society of contrary and contradictory religious and philosophical points of view, the law must address, with fairness and consistency, how public schools ought to deal with the question of origins without violating both the deliverances of science and the rights of the nation's citizens.

The infusion of Intelligent Design into this debate has changed the legal landscape significantly. Unlike the creation science repudiated by the Supreme Court in *Epperson* and *Edwards*, ID cannot be dismissed as a transparent attempt on the part of religious people to force their views on the public schools. Instead, ID advocates, if their case reaches our highest courts, will force even our most cerebral jurists to carefully and conscientiously assess a jurisprudence that up until now could be—without fear of serious inspection—papered over with the caricature of William Jennings Bryan[2] trying to figure out where Cain found his wife. This quasi-official, "Inherit the Wind" caricature has outlived its usefulness. It has, to enlist a bad pun, not evolved. ID is not your Daddy's fundamentalism.

---

1. the 1925 trial of John T. Scopes, who was found guilty of violating a Tennessee law that prohibited the teaching of evolution in public schools   2. Bryan was a fundamentalist, an expert on the Bible, and the lawyer for the prosecution in the Scopes trial. Clarence Darrow, a famous criminal lawyer who defended John Scopes, put Bryan on the stand and humiliated him by asking questions about the Bible that he could not answer.

6

Public Schools Should Teach Evolution Only

John R. Staver

John R. Staver is a professor of science education and the director for the Center for Science Education at Kansas State University in Manhattan, Kansas.

Scientific theories must undergo rigorous scrutiny and testing. Only after such examination proves the theory's ability to explain and predict can it be accepted as new scientific knowledge by the scientific community. And only then can it be introduced into a public school's curriculum. Evolution has undergone 140 years of such scrutiny and has held up as a theory that can explain the observed diversity and underlying unity of living organisms very well. It has been used to make a wide variety of accurate predictions. On the other hand, advocates of Intelligent Design (ID)—a type of creationism that its advocates claim uses scientific facts to show that life on Earth was created by an intelligent designer—have not generated acceptable scientific work to show how ID can explain or predict. ID fails to meet the requirements of scientific theory in four ways: Its advocates do not set aside explanations that are beyond human reason, as the nature of science requires; its advocates criticize and distort the character of evolution and science in general; ID cannot explain or predict as well as evolution; and the motivation, strategy, and behavior of ID advocates are not scientific. Therefore, ID should not be taught in public classrooms.

In an ideal democracy all citizens would exhibit the capacity to agree to disagree and to tolerate and respect others' views. Though democratic, our society is far from ideal, and schools often become battlegrounds over contrasting viewpoints because public education simultaneously reflects society's broad landscape of values and transmits them as it prepares future citizens.

ID and Schools

School board actions in Ohio and Georgia concerning intelligent design (ID) theory in schools display all the earmarks of arguments over whose values should be taught in science class. In December 2002, following almost a year of national publicity and debate, the Ohio State Board of Education rejected attempts to include ID in Ohio's new science standards. In September 2002, the local board of education in Georgia's second largest school district, Cobb County, approved a policy affirming the discussion of contested viewpoints in academic disciplines, citing the origin of species as an example. In January 2003, after weeks of criticism from the scientific community, the board clarified its policy by stating that controversy over evolution is a social issue. As the 2003–2004 school year opened, attempts to include ID in school science were underway in Texas and New Mexico.

> **//** *This is indeed a marathon dispute; round one took place in a Dayton, Tennessee, courtroom in 1925.* **//**

William Dembski, a leader in the ID movement, defines ID in three parts: "... a scientific research program that investigates the effects of intelligent causes; an intellectual movement that challenges Darwinism and its naturalistic legacy; and a way of understanding divine action" Michael Behe, another proponent of ID, argues that many systems within living organisms are too complex to have developed by evolutionary processes; therefore, such systems must have been designed. Behe cites the bacterial flagellum, blood clotting pathway, and immune system as examples and coined the terms "irreducible complexity" and "irreducibly complex" to describe any "... single system composed of several well-matched, interacting parts that contribute to the basic function, wherein the removal of any one of the parts causes the system to effectively cease functioning."

Advocates of ID theory argue that evolution is a theory in crisis, ID is a legitimate scientific theory, and biology teachers should teach the controversy. Supporters of evolutionary theory testify that ID is a religious, not scientific, concept, and evolution is in no danger of bankruptcy, having survived 140 years of scientific scrutiny quite well. Evolution proponents further ask to examine ID advocates' scientific research reports on ID. This is indeed a marathon dispute; round one took place in a Dayton, Tennessee, courtroom in 1925.

This article discusses the process of generating new scientific knowledge and accepting it in our schools, explains why evolution is not in crisis, documents the lack of evidence in ID theory, and recommends methods to incorporate issues surrounding evolution in the classroom.

Establishing New Knowledge

The controversy between ID and evolutionary theory raises an important question: How is the subject matter of school science determined? The first step is the acceptance of new scientific knowledge by the relevant scientific community. Such knowledge may be in the form of a theory, law, principle, hypothesis, fact, or other aspects of the nature of science. When scientists amass extensive empirical evidence that conflicts with a prevailing theory, they begin to question that theory, and at some point they propose a new theory. Scientists in relevant fields empirically test the proposed theory's capacity to explain and predict. If this work eventually confirms that the new theory explains more, predicts better, and documents the limitations of its predecessor, then scientists incorporate the new theory by replacing or substantially modifying its predecessor.

One example often recounted in high school chemistry texts is the acceptance of the quantum mechanical model of the atom from its immediate predecessor, the Bohr model, and from the earlier models of Rutherford and Thomson. British scientist J.J. Thomson drew upon his knowledge of raisin pudding to conceive negatively charged electrons—analogous to raisins—as distributed throughout a consistent, positively charged mass of atom—analogous to pudding. Thomson's model predicted that alpha particles should be deflected when passed through a thin layer of atoms.

Testing Thomson's model, Ernest Rutherford passed alpha particles through thin gold foil and found that most alpha particles were undeflected. Rutherford concluded that an atom is primarily empty space with a small, dense, positively charged mass at its center. Rutherford was unable to reconcile the electron, but Niels Bohr proposed that an electron orbits the hydrogen nucleus in a circle at quantized energy levels. Bohr's model explained the spectrum of hydrogen but failed to explain the spectra of more complex systems. Louis deBroglie argued that electrons, like light, act as both particles and waves; the heavier the mass of a particle, the more negligible the wave character of its motion. DeBroglie's prediction that electron motion would demonstrate substantial wave character was confirmed by experiments observing the diffraction of electrons. The modern quantum mechanical model of the atom takes into account the substantial wave character of electron motion. This example of how scientific work modified or replaced older models and established the currently accepted model of electron motion in atoms illustrates how scientists empirically test and modify existing knowledge to produce new knowledge. Evolutionary theory is another example. Scientists also worked—and continue to work—to test, validate, and improve evolutionary theory as a tool to explain and predict biological phenomena.

> *Once established, new scientific understandings enter school science curricula after extensive discussions and consensus building among all stakeholder groups.*

Once established, new scientific understandings enter school science curricula after extensive discussions and consensus building among all stakeholder groups. Only after both steps are completed do new scientific theories, laws, principles, facts, and additional components of the nature of science reach schools. For example, the structure, function, and replication of DNA are routinely described in today's high school biology texts, but such descriptions are absent in the Gregor Mendel edition of *Modern Biology*. Their absence in 1958 is hardly surprising; Watson and Crick only proposed their model in 1953 and did not share a Nobel Prize with Wilkins until 1962.

Development of the *National Science Education Standards (NSES)* illustrates a more recent process of discussion and consensus. Twenty-two scientific and science education societies and over 18,000 individual scientists, science educators, teachers, school administrators, and parents reviewed and critiqued the efforts of the working groups of scientists, teachers, and educators who developed the Standards over a four-year process.

Where Is the Evidence?

ID dates back to Aristotle's final cause and the Stoics' inference of God's existence from biological complexity. In 1802, the English philosopher and theologian William Paley published an argument by analogy: Just as a watch has a maker, so does the world have a maker, who is God. The modern concept of ID surfaced in 1991 when Phillip Johnson, now emeritus professor of law at the University of California at Berkeley, published *Darwin on Trial.*

> *There is no published evidence . . . that the scientific community currently views evolution as a theory in crisis, with ID being studied as a potentially viable successor.*

[More than a dozen] years have passed since Johnson subpoenaed evolution. If evolution is a theory in crisis, if scientists have proposed ID as a new theory, and if scientists in relevant fields are reporting research on the merits of ID theory, then we should find extensive empirical evidence in the form of published articles in refereed scientific research journals.

Leslie Lane, a biologist at the University of Nebraska–Lincoln, conducted an electronic search of the Science Citation Index over the 12 years [since Johnson's book]. Approximately 10,600,000 published articles were searched in 5,300 journals. "Intelligent design" was only a keyword in 88 articles; 77 of these were in various fields of engineering, exactly where one should expect design to be a prominent concept. The remaining 11 articles included 8 that criticized the scientific foundation for ID; 3 of those articles appeared in nonresearch journals. "Specified complexity" and "irreducible complexity," two important concepts of ID theory, appeared in 0 and 6 articles, respectively.

On the contrary, approximately 115,000 articles used "evolution" as a keyword, primarily referring to biological evolution, and natural selection was a keyword phrase in 4,100 articles. In summary, there is no published evidence in refereed scientific literature surveyed that supports the hypothesis that the scientific community currently views evolution as a theory in crisis, with ID being studied as a potentially viable successor.

> *// Scientists refrain from considering God's actions in their work. //*

Lane conducted another electronic search of the Science Citation Index, Social Sciences Citation Index, and Arts and Humanities Citation Index [since 1991] to examine ID advocates' admonition to teach the controversy over biological evolution within the scientific community. Approximately 13,800,000 articles were searched. Lane found only 22 articles with the keywords "creation" and "controversy," all focusing on the controversy between science and fundamentalist religion. Approximately 108,000 articles used the keyword "evolution," with perhaps one-fourth to one-third of these focusing on biological evolution. This search demonstrates that the scientific community does not view evolution as a theory in crisis. Evidence does exist, however, for a controversy over evolution between religious fundamentalism and science.

Not a Scientific Theory

ID is not a scientific theory for four reasons. First, ID's advocates do not set aside explanations that are beyond human reason, as the nature of science requires. Scientists refrain from considering God's actions in their work. Instead they use observation, experimentation, prevailing scientific theory, mathematics, logical arguments, strict empirical standards, heuristics, and healthy skepticism to produce knowledge. Scientific theories are therefore explanations about aspects of nature without reference to God. This means they are natural, and we call this context methodological naturalism.

Second, ID's advocates spend their time, resources, and energy criticizing and distorting the character of evolution in particular and science in general. One example is their claim that science practiced as methodological naturalism is atheistic. The methodological naturalism of scientific work and knowledge does not mean that scientific work and knowledge are atheistic. Let me demonstrate this point with two hypothetical science teachers, Sue and Joe. Do Sue and Joe consider God in deciding where to park their cars in the school parking lot or where to sit in a theatre? If not, Sue and Joe use methodological naturalism to make their decisions. Do Sue and Joe, then, reject God because they do not consider Him in their decisions? I think not. Scientific work and knowledge are properly silent about God because they do not consider Him. Science cannot logically conclude that God does or does not exist because science does not consider God in its work. Claims that evolution is atheistic or that science denies God are based on faulty logic, assume a particular philosophical view, or both.

> *Teachers should help students understand further that using the tools of science does not require the rejection of existing tools such as personal religious beliefs.*

The claim that evolution is a theory in crisis, perhaps even in bankruptcy, because it cannot answer certain questions is a classic example of a logical fallacy that philosophers call an appeal to ignorance. [According to American philosopher P.J. Hurley's textbook, *A Concise Introduction to Logic*,] "when the premises of an argument state that nothing has been proved one way or the other about something, and the conclusion then makes a definite assertion about that thing, the argument commits an appeal to ignorance. The issue usually involves something that is incapable of being proved or something that has not yet been proved." The further claim that ID is the only alternative to evolution involves the logical fallacy of the false dichotomy. This fallacy ". . . is committed when one premise of an argument . . . presents two alternatives . . . as if no third alternative were possible." For instance, yet another alternative states that evolution is God's design.

Third, a useful scientific theory will be modified or replaced only when a new theory is proposed and documented through scientific work to explain and predict as much or more. (I discussed this issue above in terms of how new scientific understandings reach schools.) Until this happens, ID has no place in school science.

Fourth, the motivation, strategy, and behavior of ID advocates are not scientific. This point can be clarified with a metaphor. Standing in line is perhaps a universal experience. Meal lines, grocery cashier lines, driver's license lines, and auto license plate lines are all too familiar experiences that sometimes test our patience. What do folks who are waiting in line think when someone cuts in line? Their thoughts are probably neither positive nor charitable. ID theory and its advocates are attempting to cut in line. Biological evolution stood in line over 140 years to become the single accepted scientific theory for explaining the observed diversity and underlying unity of living organisms. Standing in line means that evolution has been thoroughly and repeatedly examined through accepted scientific work, which shows that evolution explains the observed diversity and underlying unity of living organisms very well, but not completely. Standing in line also means that scientists use evolution to make an extensive variety of accurate predictions. Such work has provided humans with antibiotics, vaccines, and better foods. ID advocates have not generated acceptable scientific work, nor have they set forth accurate predictions based on their work; their theoretical proposal is to an audience of citizens, not to the scientific community. A central strategy of ID advocates' appeal to the public is to charge that scientists are unfair, biased, close-minded, and protective of a bankrupt theory. The scientific community has responded, and continues to respond, by pointing out that the advocates of ID theory are attempting to cut in line by not conducting and reporting acceptable scientific work.

Controversy in the Classroom

One question remains: How can high school science teachers apply these issues in the classroom? . . . I maintain that teachers should first know and appreciate that students come to class with a great deal of prior knowledge. Time spent learning individual students' conceptions about evolutionary concepts, cultural values, and religious backgrounds is time well invested, as teachers can reduce perceived threats of evolutionary concepts and thereby help students become more receptive to understanding worldviews alternative to their own.

Teachers should also commit to teach for understanding, not belief. Teachers need to focus on helping students understand that scientific theories and scientific inquiry are specialized tools. Teachers should help students understand further that using the tools of science does not require the rejection of existing tools such as personal religious beliefs. The earlier series of questions regarding one's consideration of personal religious views in deciding where to park the car or sit in a theatre can resolve such conflicts. . . .

Lastly, teachers should be prepared to capitalize on students' positive characteristics, their natural interests, and their demands for relevance. Teachers can accomplish this by . . . emphasizing the power, utility, and relevance of evolutionary theory as an explanatory and predictive tool.

Evolution explains the extensive diversity of living organisms across the broad landscape of the life sciences and the unity that lies underneath such diversity. Predictions based on evolution have led to numerous advances that directly affect students' personal lives. Finally, teachers should perhaps point out that somewhere today is a high school student who may eventually develop a cure for HIV. These are the reasons to include evolution in the science curriculum, teach evolution in a Standards-based manner, and aim for all students to understand evolution.

7

Evolution and Creationism Both Contribute to Human Understanding

Michael Ruse

Michael Ruse is professor of philosophy at Florida State University in Tallahassee. He is the author of numerous books, including The Darwinian Revolution, Taking Darwin Seriously, *and* Can a Darwinian Be a Christian?

Although science and religion have long been in conflict, the conflict was not always as bitter as it is today. For example, the church during the time of St. Augustine (A.D. 353–430) held the position that one read the Bible literally unless and until reason or science showed otherwise. In the nineteenth century, many devout Christians combined their faith with their science. But things were already changing. Some evolutionists very strongly rejected any and all Christianity as totally incompatible with science. And many Christians began to read the Bible extremely literally, rejecting any science (such as evolution) that was incompatible with it. Today, many evolutionists and many creationists eagerly fuel a rivalry that has come to seem like an impasse. Yet each side could benefit if they tried harder to understand each other. Science has benefited from religion in the past— as during the Reformation, when devout people explored the nature of the universe—and probably could in the future. And religion has grown stronger in the past

Michael Ruse, "Natural Selection vs. Intelligent Design," *USA Today Magazine*, vol. 132, January 2004, pp. 32–35. Copyright © 2004 by the Society for the Advancement of Education. Reproduced by permission.

due to science—as when Copernicus showed that Earth was not the center of the universe—and can continue to do so.

"Tell me, Professor Huxley, are you descended from monkeys on your grandfather's side or your grandmother's side?" This question was posed by Samuel Wilberforce, Bishop of Oxford, England, in a famous debate in 1860. It was the year after British naturalist Charles Darwin had published *On the Origin of Species*, where he argued that all organisms are the end result of a long, slow, natural process of development known as evolution. Church authorities were up in arms, and Wilberforce was debating the issue with one of the most famous scientists of the day, "Darwin's bulldog," Thomas Henry Huxley. Supposedly, Huxley retorted that he would rather be descended from a monkey than from a bishop of the Church of England. Probably he said something less biting, but it not only makes for a good story (if only in fiction), it demonstrates vividly that evolution brought on renewed conflict between science and religion.

> *We have conflict between evolution, particularly Darwinism, and Christianity, especially that version known as Creationism. Natural origin vs. six days of miracles.*

First there was Galileo Galilei. Then there was Darwin. Science and religion at war—a conflict ongoing today, particularly in America, as professional scientists endorse evolution while many Christians argue instead for a picture of life's origins based on the early chapters of Genesis. We have conflict between evolution, particularly Darwinism, and Christianity, especially that version known as Creationism. Natural origin vs. six days of miracles.

Faith and Science

Actually, history demonstrates that the facts are a little more complex and interesting. Traditionally, it was never the case that Christianity insisted on a completely literal reading of the Bible. St. Augustine (A.D. 353–430), the most influential of the early Christian theologians, knew that there were all sorts of problems if the Bible was taken literally. St. Augustine's position, adopted by the Church, is that one accepts a literal reading, unless and until reason or empirical science shows otherwise. Then one changes. The Bible—the Old Testament particularly—was written for primitive nomadic folk, not sophisticated modern thinkers, so much is expected to be metaphorical or allegorical. As it happens, St. Augustine himself felt no reason to challenge the Creation stories of Genesis, but he certainly paved the way for science to demand a revision.

> *It is no surprise that the Church—especially the Catholic Church in the Middle Ages—was no foe of science, and indeed was the place in which science was developed and cherished.*

With this kind of theological background, it is no surprise that the Church—especially the Catholic Church in the Middle Ages—was no foe of science, and indeed was the place in which science was developed and cherished. Nicholas Copernicus, the father of the heliocentric theory of the universe (sun as center, Earth circling it) was in minor orders, and died in good standing. It is true that the Protestant Reformation made the status of the Bible's literal truth more pressing. After this, Catholics responded with their Counter-Reformation. Galileo encountered resistance a century after Copernicus, precisely because he insisted that the sun is the center of things. Yet, there was room for interpretation and metaphorical readings. Protestant reformer Jean Calvin, particularly, insisted that God accommodated His language to unsophisticated readers and they must be prepared to move beyond. Calvin stressed the importance of God's working through law and of worshiping Him precisely by abiding these laws. It is no coincidence that the Reformation brought a great flowering of science, as devout people explored the nature of the mysterious and wonderful universe in which they lived.

Evolutionary ideas surfaced in the 18th century. One of the earliest thinkers in this mode was Erasmus Darwin, grandfather of Charles, and a very good friend of one of America's Founding Fathers, Benjamin Franklin. The elder Darwin was no atheist, but neither was he a Christian. Rather, he was a Deist, believing that God had set things in motion and then stood back and let all work through unbroken law. Obviously, evolution was proof of such a God rather than a threat. One should not think that this was in any way an insincere religious position, or necessarily halfway to nonbelief. For many, a god of law was as superior to a god of miracle as an industrialist who made cloth through machines was superior to a handweaver.

The Christians of the day did not subscribe to evolution, but by the first half of the 19th century, many were starting to realize that, in the light of modern science, Genesis could not be taken absolutely literally. Geology was a crucial science in the Industrial Revolution—mining as well as canal and railroad building depended on it—and it revealed that the Earth seems far more ancient than those 6,000 years of tradition, based on the genealogies given in the Old Testament. There was little proof of a universal flood either, although there was increasing evidence of a progressivist kind of fossil record, with very primitive forms at the lowest levels, and the most modern organisms at the highest levels. Although when Darwin published there were critics similar to the Bishop of Oxford who opposed evolution, as soon as Darwin said, "organisms came about through evolution," a huge number agreed.

> *The Christians of the day did not subscribe to evolution, but by the first half of the 19th century, many were starting to realize that, in the light of modern science, Genesis could not be taken absolutely literally.*

This was the case in the U.S. as well as Britain and the rest of Europe. In fact, thanks to the fabulous fossil finds from the West, America rapidly became part of the cutting edge of evolutionary studies. Rich collectors spent fortunes digging out denizens of the past, and in shipping the remains back East for display in the new museums of the growing cities.

As the century drew to a close, many devout Christians in the U.S. as well as Britain found that they could meld their faith with their science. One of the most enthusiastic evolutionists of the era was James McCosh, Presbyterian minister, and progressive president of Princeton University. He was so confident of evolution and its compatibility with the Christian faith that he sent several of his brightest students to study with Huxley—the best educator in the business—although he was anything but religious (having invented the term, "agnostic").

A Clash of Traditions

So, why then today do we have a clash between science and religion, between evolution and Christianity? For starters, the evolutionists deliberately set out to pick quarrels with the Christians and, in a way, to provide their own rival, secular tradition—one based on evolution. Visionaries like Huxley saw much need for the reformation of society—new schools, revamped technical education, streamlined bureaucracy, a military based on talent and not on privilege, and proper medical training where doctors cured rather than killed. They envisioned religion (especially in Europe) often allied with the establishment forces. Christianity was in accord with the power structure and did not want to relinquish control. Consequently, Huxley and supporters set up their rival edifice the church of science, with evolution as its foundation. . . . Can a Darwinian be a Christian? Absolutely not!

On the other hand, in the U.S. especially, there developed a tradition of ultrabiblical literalism. In a way, this turn was a bit surprising. The key figures of the American Revolution tended to take Christianity with more than a pinch of salt. For instance, George Washington never received communion, while Thomas Jefferson referred to the Trinity as "Abracadabra." However, by the early 1800s, in one of the so-called "Great Awakenings," evangelical religion swept the young nation by storm. By mid century—before the big influx of Catholics and then, later, Jews—over half the nation was church-going and 85% were evangelical Protestants, mainly Methodists and Baptists. The Bible was their guide to life, and part of the belief was that everyone was capable of reading the Good Book for guidance. The slavery issue shook the confidence of some in this attitude—both the Old and New Testaments taken literally seem to condone the practice—but even after the Civil War, many parts of the nation, especially in the South and West, continued to believe that all of the Bible, without exception, was absolutely factual.

By century's end, evolution had become a litmus test. If you were a true believer, you rejected the dreadful doctrine.

The struggle continued into the 20th century. In 1925, a test was the Scopes Monkey Trial, when a young Tennessee man was prosecuted for teaching evolution in the schools. Although his conviction was overturned on a technicality, the laws governing evolution's place—or lack thereof—stayed on the books for many years. More significantly, because of Christian opposition, evolution was taken out of all of the biology textbooks, so few students were taught the doctrine. It was only after the USSR's Sputnik launching convinced the U.S. of the need for updated science education that evolution again came to the forefront and controversy arose once more. More recently, there has been an articulate group of philosophers and scientists, from an evangelical perspective, pushing an updated form of Creationism. They call their position "Intelligent Design" and, as the name implies, it supposes that the origins of living things require supernatural interventions to create the intricate, design-like, living forms that we see all around us.

> **//** Is there any way forward from this impasse? Both sides understanding their own histories a little better would be an admirable start. **//**

Many evolutionists are no less eager to keep the old rivalries going. . . . Richard Dawkins, the English evolutionist and author of the best-selling *The Selfish Gene*, writes that a "cowardly flabbiness of the intellect afflicts otherwise rational people confronted with long-established religions." Jerry Coyne, leading Darwinian biologist at the University of Chicago, quotes George Orwell in his attack on Christianity: "One has to belong to the Intelligentsia to believe things like that. No ordinary man could be such a fool.". . .

Mutual Profit

Is there any way forward from this impasse? Both sides understanding their own histories a little better would be an admirable start. Moreover, each could make a greater effort to better consider the positions of the other. Let me elucidate.

Creationists frequently state that evolution can at best be only a theory, not a fact. Why? Most obviously, because (except in very minor and limited examples) we never see evolution actually occur. Even if birds really did evolve from dinosaurs, as many paleontologists would argue, no one was around to actually witness it. While this latter point is true, the former conclusion does not follow. Often, we believe things through circumstantial evidence. In fact, sometimes we prefer it. Take an accusation of rape. Which would more convince before convicting? An eyewitness testimony or DNA verification? Given how often witnesses are mistaken, especially at times of great tension, most would choose the DNA. We would not think it merely a theory. We would believe it enough of a fact to convict. Evolution provides a similar argument. I am not claiming that the data is always strong enough. I am saying it is unfair always to rule out indirect evidence because it is indirect.

> *The two camps could use each other to mutual profit.*

Go the other way. Evolutionists whine incessantly about Genesis. Coyne's take: "The fossil record shows that the Genesis version of creation is manifestly wrong if read literally, and one is left either questioning the authority of the Bible or recognising that it is a prolonged exercise in metaphor—and as such open to endless interpretation." What is wrong with metaphor and interpretation? Sometimes we say far more with metaphor than if we try to speak literally. Evolutionists hardly can complain about metaphors. Darwin's mechanism of evolution is "natural selection," and that is a metaphor par excellence. As is Dawkins' talk of selfish genes. People are selfish, not genes, but it does not mean that the comparison is silly, useless, or even open to "endless interpretation." (And if it is, so what? Sometimes we keep changing interpretations as circumstances evolve and as new questions arise.) Why should Christians be denied the opportunity to interpret Genesis symbolically? Although St. Augustine thought the story of Genesis true, he also felt that God stands outside time—to speak of Him as eternal does not mean everlasting, but beyond time. Hence, for God, the thought, the act, and the product of creation were as one. St. Augustine thought that God created seeds that develop, in time, into living things. This may not have been exactly what we might mean by evolutionary, but it is a philosophy that seems to lend itself to evolution—and there cannot be a much more traditional Christian than St. Augustine.

The real point is that the two camps could use each other to mutual profit. Science does not have all of the answers, and modesty about its limits would not be such a bad thing. Science has owed much to religion in the past. Perhaps this could be true of the future as well.

Conversely, religion cannot and should not stand still. The Copernican Revolution may have been uncomfortable, but realizing that we are not the center of a tight little universe is a challenge that can only make religion stronger. The same can be true of evolution. Suppose there was no literal Adam or Eve. The idea of original sin is not necessarily lost. Perhaps Dawkins' selfish genes can tell us something, namely, that built into our nature is something that brings on selfishness, something that we must strive to overcome. We are as we are, not because one man and one woman ate a forbidden apple, but because of our biology. I am not saying this is necessarily so. I would say this makes a lot more moral sense. No longer are we responsible for someone else's actions, but just our own. Agree or not, I maintain that an evolutionary perspective on life is an exciting prospect for the Christian to explore. We may see through a glass darkly, but nothing in the Bible forbids an attempt to clean that glass a little.

Organizations to Contact

The editors have compiled the following list of organizations concerned with the issues debated in this book. The descriptions are derived from materials provided by the organizations. All have publications or information available for interested readers. The list was compiled on the date of publication of the present volume; names, addresses, phone and fax numbers, and e-mail addresses may change. Be aware that many organizations take several weeks or longer to respond to inquiries, so allow as much time as possible.

American Institute of Biological Sciences (AIBS)
1444 I St. NW, Suite 200, Washington, DC 20005
(202) 628-1500 • fax: (202) 628-1509
Web site: www.aibs.org

AIBS is an umbrella organization of scientific professional societies. It provides services, support, and a voice for a variety of biological disciplines. AIBS promotes biological research and education, disseminates research findings, and advises policy makers in Congress and the private sector. It supports the teaching of evolution and opposes the teaching of creationism in science education. It publishes the monthly magazine *Bioscience.*

American Scientific Affiliation (ASA)
PO Box 668, Ipswich, MA 01938
(978) 356-5656 • fax: (978) 356-4375
e-mail: asa@asa3.org • Web site: www.asa3.org/ASA

ASA is a fellowship of Christian scientists. The organization supports modern scientific research but weighs both scientific and biblical insights in questions regarding natural phenomena, historical events such as creation, and the place of Christianity in scientific ideas. Its publications include the *American Scientific Affiliation Newsletter* and *Perspectives on Science and Christian Faith.*

Creation Research Society (CRS)
PO Box 8263, St. Joseph, MO 64508-8263
e-mail: contact@creationresearch.org
Web site: www.creationresearch.org

CRS is a society of Christians who believe that the facts of science support the revealed account of creation in the Bible. The society maintains the Van Andel Research Center, a laboratory-equipped facility in Arizona, to facilitate and support the scientific study of the theories of creation and evolution. CRS conducts research and disseminates information to the public. Publications include the technical journal *CRS Quarterly* and a bimonthly newsletter, *Creation Matters.*

Discovery Institute's Center for Science and Culture (CSC)
1511 Third Ave., Suite 808, Seattle, WA 98101
(206) 292-0401 • fax: (206) 682-5320
e-mail: cscinfo@discovery.org • Web site: www.discovery.org/csc

The Discovery Institute is a public policy organization that publicizes and promotes belief in representative government, the free market, and individual liberty. Fellows submit their analyses and proposals to public discourse through books, articles, legislative testimony, seminars, conferences, and debates, as well as the institute's Web site. A specific program of the Discovery Institute, the Center for Science and Culture, supports research into Intelligent Design theory and challenges aspects of Darwinism, and encourages schools to include Intelligent Design in science curricula.

Genesis Institute (GI)
740 South 128th St., Seattle, WA 98168-2728
e-mail: whjlang@juno.com • Web site: www.creationism.org/lang

GI is made up of individuals seeking to publicize the value of the Gospel in sciences and bring the Bible and science together. It stresses Creation Evangelism and believes that the universe is less than six thousand years old. It conducts educational and research programs and offers home schooling program materials.

Institute of Human Origins (IHO)
Arizona State University, PO Box 874101, Tempe, AZ 85287-4101
(480) 727-6580 • fax: (480) 727-6570
e-mail: iho@asu.edu • Web site: www.asu.edu/clas/iho

The institute comprises scientists, educators, students, volunteers, and other individuals carrying out research supporting human evolution. It utilizes the expertise and knowledge of many disciplines to establish when, where, and how the human species originated. It promotes laboratory and field research and advises researchers from project planning stages to the dissemination of results. It offers specialized training to scientists and students and maintains an archive of statistics, photographs, slides, casts, field notes, and comparative collections.

National Academy of Sciences (NAS)
500 Fifth St. NW, Washington, DC 20001
(202) 334-2000
Web site: www.nas.edu

The NAS is a private, honorary organization dedicated to the furthering of science and engineering; members are elected in recognition of their distinguished and continuing contributions to either of the two fields. It was founded by an act of Congress to serve as official adviser to the federal government on scientific and technical matters. It advocates the teaching of evolution as a central element in any science education program. Its publications include *Biographical Memoirs* and the monthly *Proceedings of the National Academy of Sciences*.

National Center for Science Education (NCSE)
420 Fortieth St., Suite 2, Oakland, CA 94609-2509
(510) 601-7203 • fax: (510) 601-7204
e-mail: ncseoffice@ncseweb.org • Web site: www.natcenscied.org

NCSE is an affiliate of the American Association for the Advancement of Science, one of the world's largest scientific societies. It is made up of scientists, teachers, students, clergy, and interested individuals, who seek to improve science education, specifically the study of evolutionary science, and oppose the teaching of creationism in public school science curricula. It publishes books, pamphlets, and audio and videocassettes on evolution education and education on the nature of scientific inquiry. It also publishes *Reports of the National Center for Science Education.*

National Science Teachers Association (NSTA)
1840 Wilson Blvd., Arlington, VA 22201-3000
(703) 243-7100
Web site: www.nsta.org

NSTA membership comprises teachers seeking to foster excellence in science teaching. The association sponsors studies into how students learn, the science curriculum, teaching preparation, and classroom and laboratory procedures and facilities. The NSTA strongly supports the position that evolution is a major unifying concept in science and should be integral to K–12 science education. It supports the view that science teachers should not advocate any religious interpretations of nature and should be nonjudgmental about the personal beliefs of students. Publications include *Journal of College Science Teaching* and *Reports on the Teaching of Science at the College Level.* It also publishes curriculum development and professional materials, teaching aids, career booklets, and audiovisual aids.

Reasons to Believe (RTB)
PO Box 5978, Pasadena, CA 91117
(800) 482-7836 • (626) 335-1480 • fax: (626) 852-0178
e-mail: reasons@reasons.org • Web site: www.reasons.org

RTB seeks to explain the theory of Creation as both biblically sound and scientifically valid, in an effort to remove the doubts of religious skeptics and strengthen the faith of Christians. It conducts research and educational programs and operates a speakers bureau. Its publications include the quarterly newsletter *Facts and Faith.*

Bibliography

Books

Vine Deloria — *Evolution, Creationism, and Other Modern Myths: A Critical Inquiry.* Golden, CO: Fulcrum, 2002.

William A. Dembski — *No Free Lunch: Why Specified Complexity Cannot Be Purchased Without Intelligence.* Lanham, MD: Rowman & Littlefield, 2001.

William A. Dembski — *Uncommon Dissent: Intellectuals Who Find Darwinism Unconvincing.* Wilmington, DE: ISI Books, 2004.

William A. Dembski and Michael Ruse, eds. — *Debating Design: From Darwin to DNA.* New York: Cambridge University Press, 2004.

Niles Eldredge — *The Triumph of Evolution: And the Failure of Creationism.* New York: W.H. Freeman, 2000.

Barbara Carroll Forrest and Paul R. Gross — *Creationism's Trojan Horse: The Wedge of Intelligent Design.* Oxford, UK: Oxford University Press, 2003.

Karl W. Giberson and Donald A. Yerxa — *Species of Origins: America's Search for a Creation Story.* Lanham, MD: Rowman & Littlefield, 2002.

Langdon Brown Gilkey — *Blue Twilight: Nature, Creationism, and American Religion.* Minneapolis, MN: Fortress, 2001.

Zachary Hayes — *The Gift of Being: A Theology of Creation.* Collegeville, MN: Liturgical, 2001.

Cornelius G. Hunter — *Darwin's God: Evolution and the Problem of Evil.* Grand Rapids, MI: Brazos, 2001.

Steve Jones — *Darwin's Ghost: The Origin of Species Updated.* New York: Ballantine, 2001.

David C. Lindberg and Ronald L. Numbers — *When Science and Christianity Meet.* Chicago: University of Chicago Press, 2003.

Kenneth R. Miller — *Finding Darwin's God: A Scientist's Search for Common Ground Between God and Evolution.* New York: HarperCollins, 1999.

National Academy of Sciences — *Science and Creationism: A View from the National Academy of Sciences.* Washington, DC: National Academies Press, 1999.

Robert T. Pennock — *The Tower of Babel.* Cambridge, MA: MIT Press, 1999.

Mark Perakh	*Untintelligent Design*. Amherst, NY: Prometheus, 2004.
Michael C. Rea	*World Without Design: The Ontological Consequences of Naturalism*. Oxford, UK: Oxford University Press, 2002.
Michael Ruse	*Can a Darwinian Be a Christian? The Relationship Between Science and Religion*. Cambridge, MA: Harvard University Press, 2000.
Michael Ruse	*Darwin and Design: Does Evolution Have a Purpose?* Cambridge, MA: Harvard University Press, 2003.
Gerald L. Schroeder	*The Hidden Face of God: How Science Reveals the Ultimate Truth*. New York: Free Press, 2001.
Geoffrey Simmons	*What Darwin Didn't Know*. Eugene, OR: Harvest House, 2004.
James W. Skehan	*The Creation Controversy & the Science Classroom: Modern Science and the Book of Genesis*. Arlington, VA: NSTA Press, 2000.
Lee Strobel	*The Case for a Creator: A Journalist Investigates Scientific Evidence That Points Toward God*. Grand Rapids, MI: Zondervan, 2004.
Tom Vail	*Grand Canyon: A Different View*. Green Forest, AZ: Master, 2003.
Richard Weikart	*From Darwin to Hitler: Evolutionary Ethics, Eugenics, and Racism in Germany*. New York: Palgrave Macmillan, 2004.
Jonathan Wells	*Icons of Evolution: Science or Myth?* Washington, DC: Regnery, 2000.
Larry Witham	*By Design: Science and the Search for God*. San Francisco: Encounter, 2003.
Larry Witham	*Where Darwin Meets the Bible: Creationists and Evolutionists in America*. Oxford, UK: Oxford University Press, 2002.
Thomas Woodward	*Doubts About Darwin: A History of Intelligent Design*. Grand Rapids, MI: Baker, 2003.
Carl Zimmer	*Evolution: The Triumph of an Idea*. New York: HarperCollins, 2001.

Periodicals

| Francis J. Beckwith | "Science and Religion Twenty Years After *McLean v. Arkansas*: Evolution, Public Education, and the New Challenge of Intelligent Design," *Harvard Journal of Law & Public Policy*, Spring 2003. |
| David Berlinski | "A Scientific Scandal," *Commentary*, April 2003. |

Marshall Berman — "Intelligent Design Creationism: A Threat to Society—Not Just Science," *American Biology Teacher*, November/December 2003.

Robert Camp — "'Teach the Controversy': An Intelligently Designed Ruse," *Skeptical Inquirer*, September/October 2004.

James T. Costa — "Teaching Darwin with Darwin," *Bioscience*, November 2003.

Richard Dawkins — "Who Owns the Argument from Improbability?" *Free Inquiry*, October/November 2004.

Robin Dunbar — "Evolution: Five Big Questions," *New Scientist*, June 14, 2003.

John Garvey — "Intelligent Design," *Commonweal*, May 9, 2003.

Ron Good — "Evolution and Creationism: One Long Argument," *American Biology Teacher*, September 2003.

Paul R. Gross — "Intelligent Design and That Vast Right-Wing Conspiracy," *Scientific Insights*, September 2003.

Rich Heffern — "'Promise' of the Universe," *National Catholic Reporter*, December 12, 2003.

Phillip E. Johnson — "Intelligent Design, Freedom, and Education," *BreakPoint WorldView*, May 2003.

Bruce Martin and Frances Martin — "Neither Intelligent nor Designed," *Skeptical Inquirer*, November/December 2003.

Stephen C. Meyer — "Teach the Controversy," *Cincinnati Enquirer*, March 10, 2001.

Stephen C. Meyer — "The Origin of Biological Information and the Higher Taxonomic Categories," *Proceedings of the Biological Society of Washington*, vol. 117, no. 2, 2004.

Richard Milner and Vittorio Maestro, eds. — "Intelligent Design?" *Natural History*, April 2002.

Randy Moore — "The Dark Side of Creationism," *American Biology Teacher*, February 2004.

Mark Perakh — "The Anthropic Principle and the Big Bang: Natural or Supernatural? A Simple Probablistic Answer," *Skeptical Inquirer*, September/October 2004.

Gregory R. Peterson — "The Intelligent-Design Movement: Science or Ideology?" *Zygon*, March 2002.

Massimo Pigliucci — "The Sin of Scientism," *Skeptical Inquirer*, November/December 2003.

Evan Ratliffe — "The Crusade Against Evolution," *Wired*, October 2004.

Mark Ryland   "The Evolution Debate: Myth, Science, Culture, Education," *Today*, August 21, 2003.

Lawrence C.   "The Risk of Intelligent Design," *Science Teacher*,
Sharmann   November 2003.

Jonathan Wells   "Survival of the Fakest," *American Spectator*, December 2000/January 2001.

Jonathan Witt   "The Gods Must Be Tidy!" *Touchstone*, July/August 2004.

Index

ion

[